The Complete Sous Vide Cookbook

For Beginners and Advanced

Sophie Hayes

Warning-Disclaimer

The purpose of this book is to educate and entertain. The author or publisher does not guarantee that anyone following the techniques, suggestions, tips, ideas, or strategies will become successful. The author and publisher shall have neither liability or responsibility to anyone concerning any loss or damage caused, or alleged to be caused, directly or indirectly by the information contained in this book.

Contents

Introduction

The perfect meal is for families and togetherness, and the best way to gather your family is at the dining table. It provides a chance for you and your close ones to eat together, but most importantly to spend time together. And if your life is about spending time with those that you love, then you might want to prepare something new and delicious for your loved ones.

Human beings have always had a special relationship with food. We need it to stay alive, but it doesn't stop there – people love to eat. We all love the subtle flavor and texture of our favorite meals. And after a long day's work, we are looking forward to a nice bowl of homemade meal that melts in the mouth. Food makes us happy and can to form strong bonds between us. Preparation of food is a real art turned into everyday pleasure.

Food preparation and cooking has a long tradition and it is an inevitable part of our lives. This tradition still lives in modern times when the development of new technology has brought us some new methods of preparing a wonderfully delicious meal for our family while simplifying the entire process and saving us lots of time.

Food preparation like cooking, baking, fermentation, frying, and other methods are merely an appliance of the laws of organic chemistry and biochemistry. It means that under particular circumstances, different chemical reactions and transformations are defining the color, taste, and the texture of the food.

You should have in mind that there is a big difference between precise cooking principles and the one we all apply, and cook until set. We can talk about the real and practical application of science when a repeatable result is established under specific conditions – and when we always know what results to expect. Cooking en sous vide is a perfect example of a scientific cooking method. This extravagant cooking method has become very popular in the past couple of years. It started as a luxurious culinary trick in a famous and expensive restaurant. However, thanks to its efficiency and results, this beautiful kitchen gadget found its place in many households in the world.

The modern era of sous vide cooking starts in the early '70s in France. French chef, Georges Pralus was searching for the unique method on how to prevent the loss of juices contained within the meat. He applied the sous vide cooking technique and noticed that the taste and the texture of the meat are much better than compared to regular food preparation methods. These incredible results started a long story of sous vide.

Sous Vide cooking method is far more straightforward than you might think. Furthermore, this technique is a fascinating and exciting way to prepare a perfectly cooked meal. To cook en sous vide, you need a special water bath in a device that enables circulating, heating, and control of the water temperature. The circulation enables the equalization of the temperature in the whole dish without any oscillations. It holds the constant temperature during the entire cooking process. Some fancy and advanced versions of the device come with the case and they are very similar to bread baking machines.

The whole method is based on vacuuming ingredients in Ziploc bags. You can cook anything – from different types of meat, fish, seafood, eggs, and vegetables. Once you have combined the ingredients in the bag, you only have to submerge it in a water bath and cook at the precise temperature during the precise cooking period. This precision is exactly what makes sous vide a brilliant cooking technique.

The benefits of sous vide

I always thought that professional chefs have some special tricks or secrets when they are preparing a steak. How come they always get a perfect piece of pink meat, not just in the middle, but around the edges too? Their chicken is juicy, vegetables full of flavor, while the fish is perfectly cooked inside and outside.

Well, **the secret** is in the cooking method and accuracy - two attributes only sous vide can proudly wear. It comes from the French expression for „in the vacuum". Sometimes it is called the „Bain Marie" of the 21st century. Bain Maire is an ancient scientific method of heating the materials gradually and gently. This practical method easily found its way in the kitchen and became an inspiration for different recipes – from perfectly melted chocolate to baking a traditional cheesecake.

So, what is it about the sous vide and why this method is so revolutionary and extremely popular?

The most common problems with some standard preparation and cooking methods are the thermal process and the temperature. For example, if the temperature is too low, we are taking a massive risk of bacteria and poisoning. Too high temperature, on the other hand, might turn a beautiful piece of meat into a dry, burnt, and inedible meal.

I dare to say that the most significant benefit and advantage of the sous vide cooking technique is a low temperature. Unlike other cooking methods, the minimum temperature in sous vide keeps the flavor, color, and the texture of your food. The secret lies in the precise temperature which is established while some of the ingredients are going through protein denaturation. This means that the result will always be completely predictable and the food will be the same each time you cook it. At the end of the cooking process, some ingredients are exposed to high heat to achieve the Maillard reaction. This simple trick is applied in many different sous vide recipes to emphasize the mouthwatering aromas and vibrant colors of the ingredients.

The Maillard reaction, in a simple language, is browning the food. When cooking over 220 degrees F, a connection between sugars and proteins creates a new molecule – and that's where the unique flavors and aromas come from. This is why fried foods taste so irresistible and more delicious than the cooked ones. Maillard reaction can be achieved at higher temperatures, but this often leads to burning which creates dangerous substances.

Evenly cooked ingredients with sous vide cooking method are a perfect combination with the Maillard reaction at the end of the process. Just picture the steak, juicy from the inside but crisp and golden brown from the outside. Mouthwatering, right?

So, the **main benefits** of sous vide cooking would be:

- The **exact temperature** and thermal processing of each ingredient;
- **Perfect preservation** of natural liquids and juices within the ingredients

- **Preservation of valuable nutrients**;

- **Better penetration** of spices and herbs into the tissue;

- **Repeatability** of the results;

- **Accuracy**.

Some experts believe that the sous vide cooking method is dangerous because the food is not heated enough to destroy all the bacteria. However, the sous vide method belongs to a full spectrum of molecular gastronomy. Based on chemical and physical changes of the ingredients, chemical gastronomy is still one of the biggest trends in the culinary world. Elite chefs and masters promote sous vide method in using scientific methods and tools in food preparation. Not only that the sous vide technique destroys all the harmful bacteria, but this unique culinary method also preserves all the nutrients contained naturally within the food.

How to use it?

You don't have to be a skilled chef to use sous vide in your kitchen. Usually, it only involves three simple steps:

Attach the precision cooker to a pot of water and set the temperature and the time of cooking. A precision cooker's biggest advantage is that it doesn't require much space. This appliance is much cheaper than a microwave-sized water oven and it comes with some handy additions like WI-FI that allows you to supervise your meal from a distance. This can be particularly practical for busy schedules where you can practically cook your meal from work. Besides, less time you spend in the kitchen, more time you get to spend with your loved ones!

Investing more money in a high-quality precision cooker has so many advantages. These usually come with increased pump speed that allows you to cook a perfectly precise meal for a larger group of people. I'm sure you'll find it quite useful for all sorts of family get-togethers where each guest gets the same meal. Furthermore, investing more money means you get a smart device that even has a voice-controlled cooking option. This fabulous feature allows you complete hands-free cooking of beautiful, restaurant-like meals.

These smart Sous Vide cooking devices are elementary to use. They involve three simple steps:

- Attach the precision cooker to a pot. These cookers are suitable for all pot sizes so any deep cooking pot you have on hand will do the job. Use the adjustable clamp on the device to seal it.

- Now you have to set up the time and the temperature of your cooking. This depends on the types of food you're preparing. Use the charts below for precise cooking. Furthermore, you can connect the device to your phone using an online application and monitor your cooking from a distance. In my opinion, it's a time-saving option where you can leave your meal and walk away!

- Place a vacuum bag in the pot and pour in enough water to cover the bag. The circulation of water will ensure an even temperature throughout the entire cooking process.

Place the food in plastic Ziploc bags. The second most crucial part of sous vide cooking. As I said earlier, the secret of perfectly cooked sous vide meal lies in vacuum bags that seal the meal during a gentle water bath. Combine your ingredients such as meat, fish, poultry, vegetables, and other in an appropriate Ziploc bag and seal the lid. Spices and herbs will penetrate ingredients and bag will keep the moisture and juices.

If you don't have a vacuum sealer, you can use a simple water immersion technique or a straw. A water immersion technique is a perfect option to create a vacuum sealed bag without a vacuum sealer. Place the food in a zipper and slowly lower the bagged food into a bowl of water. The pressure of the water will press air through the top of the bag and create a vacuum you need for sous vide cooking. Another great option is to use reusable silicone bags that you can quickly clean and store after use. However, most chefs agree that a secret of sous vide cooking is not in the vacuum bags, but the temperature control. Only a precise temperature can give you desired results – and this can only be achieved with a high-quality precision cooker.

Give the meal a finishing touch of Maillard reaction. As I have already mentioned, the Maillard reaction will give a colorful picture and mouthwatering aroma to previously prepared sous vide meal. Grilling, browning, or searing will provide a n excellent and crispy golden exterior you wish to see on your plate. This combination will transform a simple meal into a poetry of flavors for the entire family.

The Ultimate Sous Vide Cooking Chart

Meat	Temperature (°F)	Time
Beef Steak, rare	129	1 hr 30 min
Beef Steak, medium-rare	136	1 hr 30min
Beef Steak, well done	158	1 hr 30min
Beef Roast, rare	133	7 hrs
Beef Roast, medium-rare	140	6 hrs
Beef Roast, well done	158	5 hrs
Beef Tough Cuts, rare	136	24 hrs
Beef Tough Cuts, medium-rare	149	16 hrs
Beef Tough Cuts, well done	185	8 hrs
Lamb Tenderloin, Ribeye, T-bone, Cutlets	134	4 hrs
Lamb Roast, Leg	134	10 hrs
Lamb Flank Steak, Brisket	134	12 hrs
Pork Chop, rare	136	1 hr
Pork Chop, medium-rare	144	1 hr
Pork Chop, well done	158	1 hr
Pork Roast, rare	136	3 hrs
Pork Roast, medium-rare	144	3 hrs
Pork Roast, well done	158	3 hrs
Pork Tough Cuts, rare	144	16 hrs
Pork Tough Cuts, medium-rare	154	12 hrs
Pork Tough Cuts, well done	154	8 hrs
Pork Tenderloin	134	1 hr 30min
Pork Baby Back Ribs	165	6 hrs
Pork Cutlets	134	5 hrs

Pork Spare Ribs	160	12 hrs
Pork Belly (quick)	185	5 hrs
Pork Belly (slow)	167	24 hrs
Chicken White Meat, super-supple	140	2 hrs
Chicken White Meat, tender and juicy	149	1 hr
Chicken White Meat, well done	167	1 hr
Chicken Breast, bone in	146	2 hrs 30 min
Chicken Breast, boneless	146	1 hr
Turkey Breast, bone in	146	4 hrs
Turkey Breast, boneless	146	2 hrs 30 min
Duck Breast	134	1 hr 30 min
Chicken Dark Meat, tender	149	1 hr 30 min
Chicken Dark Meat, falling off the bone	167	1 hr 30 min
Chicken Leg or Thigh, bone in	165	4 hrs
Chicken Thigh, boneless	165	1 hr
Turkey Leg or Thigh	165	2 hrs
Duck Leg	165	8 hrs
Split Game Hen	150	6 hrs
Fish, tender	104	40 min
Fish, tender and flaky	122	40 min
Fish, well done	140	40 min
Salmon, Tuna, Trout, Mackerel, Halibut, Snapper, Sole	126	30 min
Lobster	140	50 min
Scallops	140	50 min

Shrimp	140	35 min
Vegetables, root (carrots, potato, parsnips, beets, celery root, turnips)	183	3 hrs
Vegetables, tender (asparagus, broccoli, cauliflower, fennel, onions, pumpkin, eggplant, green beans, corn)	183	1 hr
Vegetables, greens (kale, spinach, collard greens, Swiss chard)	183	5 min
Fruit, firm (apple, pear)	183	45 min
Fruit, for puree	185	30 min
Fruit, berries for topping to desserts (blueberries, blackberries, raspberries, strawberries, cranberries)	154	30 min

The chart is based on the refrigerator temperature. If you're cooking frozen foods, add 15 more minutes. The size is standard and universal for all tender cuts.

Meat, Fish and Seafood

Flank Steak with Tomato Roast

(Prep + Cook Time: 2 hours 30 minutes | Serves: 3)

NUTRITIONAL INFO PER SERVING:

Calories: 71, Protein: 24g, Carbs: 5g, Fats: 4.2g

INGREDIENTS:

1 lb Flank Steak

4 tbsp Olive Oil, divided

2 tbsp Italian Seasoning

½ tsp Salt, divided into two

½ tsp Black Pepper

2 cloves Garlic, crushed

2 cloves whole Garlic

1 cup Cherry Tomatoes

1 tbsp Balsamic Vinegar

3 tbsp Parmesan Cheese, grated

DIRECTIONS:

1. Place the steak in a vacuum-sealable bag. Add half of the olive oil, 1 tbsp of Italian seasoning, black pepper, salt, and crushed garlic and rub gently.
2. Seal and submerge the bag in the water bath. Cook en sous vide for 2 hours at 129 degrees F.
3. Preheat an oven to 400 F about 10 minutes before the timer has stopped,
4. In a bowl, toss tomatoes with the remaining listed ingredients except for the Parmesan cheese. Pour into a baking dish and place in the oven on the farthest rack from the fire. Bake for 15 minutes.
5. Once the Sous Vide timer has stopped, remove the bag, unseal and remove the steak. Place the steak on flat surface and sear both sides with a torch until golden brown. Cool steak and slice thinly. Serve steak with tomato roast. Garnish with Parmesan cheese.

Prime Rib with Celery Herb Crust

(Prep + Cook Time: 5 hours 15 minutes | Serves: 3)

NUTRITIONAL INFO PER SERVING:

Calories: 112, Protein: 10.9g, Carbs: 3g, Fats: 7.3g

INGREDIENTS:

1 ½ lb Rib Eye Steak, bone in
½ tsp Black Pepper Powder
½ tsp Pink Pepper Powder
½ tbsp Celery Seeds, dried

1 tbsp Garlic Powder
2 sprigs Rosemary, minced
2 cups Beef Stock
1 Egg White

DIRECTIONS:

1. Rub salt into the meat and marinate for 1 hour.
2. Place beef in a vacuum-sealable bag, release air by the water displacement method and seal the bag.
3. Submerge the bag in the water bath.
4. Set the timer to 4 hours and cook at 130 degrees F.
5. Once the timer has stopped, remove the bag and remove the beef. Pat dry beef and place aside.
6. Mix the black pepper powder, pink pepper powder, celery seeds, garlic powder, and rosemary.
7. Brush the beef with the egg white.
8. Dip the beef in the celery seed mixture to coat graciously.
9. Place beef on a baking sheet and bake in an oven for 15 minutes.
10. Remove and allow to cool on a cutting board. Gently slice the beef, cutting against the bone.
11. Pour liquid in a vacuum bag and beef broth in a pan and bring to boil over medium heat.
12. Discard floating fat or solids.
13. Place beef slices on a plate and drizzle sauce over it.
14. Serve with a side of steamed green vegetables.

Veal Gravy

(Prep + Cook Time: 3 hours | Serves: 3)

NUTRITIONAL INFO PER SERVING:

Calories: 120, Protein: 12.1g, Carbs: 1.3g, Fats: 4.8g

INGREDIENTS:

½ lb Veal Cutlets

1 tsp Garlic Salt

1 cup Mushrooms, thinly sliced

⅓ cup Heavy Cream

2 Shallots, thinly sliced

1 tbsp Unsalted Butter

1 tsp Black Pepper Powder

1 sprig Thyme Leaves

1 tbsp Chopped Chives for garnishing

DIRECTIONS:

1. Prepare a water bath and place the Sous Vide Cooker in it.
2. Set the Sous Vide Cooker to 135 F.
3. Rub the cutlets with the garlic salt and place the veal with all the remaining listed ingredients except the chives in a vacuum-sealable bag.
4. Release the air by the water displacement method and seal it.
5. Submerge it in the water bath.
6. Cook for 2 hours 40 minutes and cook.
7. Once the timer has stopped, remove the bag and take out the veal unto a plate.
8. Transfer the sauce to a pan, discard the thyme and simmer over low heat for 5 minutes.
9. Add the veal and cook for 3 minutes.
10. Garnish with chives.
11. Serve with a side of green vegetables or bread.

Jalapeno–Tomato Rib Roast

(Prep + Cook Time: 3 hours 35 minutes | Serves: 4)

NUTRITIONAL INFO PER SERVING:

Calories: 250, Protein: 26g, Carbs: 2g, Fats: 15g

INGREDIENTS:

3 lb Beef Ribs, cut into 2

1 tsp Salt

1 tsp Black Pepper

½ cup Jalapeno–Tomato Blend

½ cup Barbecue Sauce

DIRECTIONS:

1. Rub salt and pepper graciously rib rack.
2. Put the meat in a vacuum-sealable bag, release air and seal it.
3. Cook en sous vide for 3 hours at 140 degrees F.
4. Once the timer has stopped, remove and unseal the bag.
5. Mix the remaining listed ingredients.
6. Let ribs cool for 30 minutes.
7. Meanwhile, preheat a grill on medium heat.
8. Coat ribs with the jalapeno sauce and place it on the grill.
9. Sear for 2 minutes on all sides.

Veal Chops

(Prep + Cook Time: 3 hours 10 minutes | Serves: 4)

NUTRITIONAL INFO PER SERVING:

Calories: 520, Protein: 57g, Carbs: 3.4g, Fats: 17g

INGREDIENTS:

2 (16 oz) Veal Steaks

2 tsp Salt

2 tsp Black Pepper Powder

2 tbsp Olive Oil

DIRECTIONS:

1. Prepare a water bath, place the Sous Vide Cooker in it, and set to 135 degrees F. Rub the veal with pepper and salt and place in a Ziploc bag.
2. Release air by the water displacement method and seal the bag. Submerge the bag in the water bath. Cook for 3 hours. Once the timer has stopped, remove and unseal the bag.
3. Remove the veal, pat dry using a napkin, and rub with the olive oil. Preheat a cast iron on high heat for 5 minutes.
4. Place the steak in and sear to deeply brown on both sides. Remove to a serving board. Serve with a side of salad.

Soy Garlic Tri-Tip Steak

(Prep + Cook Time: 2 hours 10 minutes | Serves: 2)

NUTRITIONAL INFO PER SERVING:

Calories: 371, Protein: 37.7g, Carbs: 5g, Fats: 14.3g

INGREDIENTS:

1 ½ lb Tri-tip Steak

Salt to taste

Pepper to taste

2 tbsp Soy Sauce

6 cloves Garlic, pre-roasted and crushed

DIRECTIONS:

1. Make a water bath, place in your Sous Vide machine, and set to 130 degrees F.
2. Season the steak with pepper and salt and place in a vacuum-sealable bag. Add the soy sauce and garlic.
3. Release air by the water displacement method and seal the bag.
4. Dip it in the water bath and set the timer for 2 hours.
5. Once the timer has stopped, remove and unseal the bag.
6. Heat a cast iron pan over high heat, place the steak in and sear on both sides for 2 minutes each. Slice and serve in a salad.

Sirloin Steaks with Mushroom Cream Sauce

(Prep + Cook Time: 1 hour 30 minutes | Serves: 3)

NUTRITIONAL INFO PER SERVING:

Calories: 220, Protein: 19.9g, Carbs: 3.9g, Fats: 6.8g

INGREDIENTS:

3 (6-oz) Boneless Sirloin Steaks
Salt and black pepper to taste
4 tsp Unsalted Butter
1 tbsp Olive Oil
6 oz Mushrooms, quartered
2 large Shallots, minced
2 cloves Garlic, minced
½ cup Beef Stock
½ cup Heavy Cream
2 tsp Mustard Sauce
Sliced Scallions for garnishing

DIRECTIONS:

1. Prepare a water bath, place Sous Vide cooker in it, and set to 135 degrees F.
2. Season the beef with pepper and salt and place in 3 separate vacuum-sealable bags.
3. Add 1 teaspoon of butter to each bag.
4. Release air by the water displacement method, seal and submerge the bags in the water bath. Cook for 1 hour.
5. Ten minutes before the timer stops, heat oil and the remaining butter in a skillet over medium heat.
6. Once the timer has stopped, remove and unseal the bags.
7. Pat dry the meat, and add to the skillet.
8. Reserve the juices in the bags.
9. Sear on each side for 1 minute and transfer to cutting board. Slice and set aside.
10. In the same skillet, add the shallots and mushrooms.
11. Cook for 10 minutes and add the garlic. Cook for 1 minute.
12. Pour in the stock and reserved juices. Simmer for 3 minutes.

13. Add in the heavy cream, bring to a boil on high heat and reduce to low heat after 5 minutes.
14. Turn the heat off and stir in the mustard sauce.
15. Place the steak on a plate, top with mushroom sauce and garnish with scallions.

Beef Pear Steak

(Prep + Cook Time: 3 hours 10 minutes | Serves: 3)

NUTRITIONAL INFO PER SERVING:

Calories: 360, Protein: 27g, Carbs: 5g, Fats: 11.5g

INGREDIENTS:

3 Beef Pear Steaks

2 tbsp Olive Oil

4 tbsp Unsalted Butter

4 cloves Garlic, crushed

4 sprigs Fresh Thyme

DIRECTIONS:

1. Make a water bath, place the Sous Vide Cooker in it, and set to 135 degrees F.
2. Season the beef with salt and place in 3 vacuum-sealable bags.
3. Release air by the water displacement method and seal bag.
4. Submerge the bags in the water bath. Cook for 3 hours.
5. Once the timer has stopped, remove the beef, pat dry, and season with pepper and salt.
6. Add oil to skillet and preheat it on medium heat until the oil starts to smoke.
7. Add the steaks, butter, garlic, and thyme. Sear for 3 minutes on both side.
8. Baste with some more butter as you cook.
9. Slice steaks into desired slices.

Ground Beef Stew

(Prep + Cook Time: 90 minutes | Serves: 3)

NUTRITIONAL INFO PER SERVING:

Calories: 274, Protein: 12.7g, Carbs: 11.4g, Fats: 21.2

INGREDIENTS:

3 eggplants

½ cup lean ground beef

1 medium-sized tomato

¼ cup extra virgin olive oil

2 tbsp toasted almonds, chopped

1 tbsp celery leaves, chopped

1 tsp salt

¼ tsp ground black pepper

DIRECTIONS:

1. Slice eggplants in half, lengthwise.
2. Remove the flesh and transfer to a bowl.
3. Generously sprinkle with salt and let stand for 10 minutes.
4. Heat three tablespoons of oil over medium-high heat.
5. Briefly fry the eggplants, for three minutes on each side and remove from the frying pan.
6. Use some kitchen paper to soak up excess oil. Set aside.
7. Now add the ground beef to the same frying pan.
8. Stir-fry for 5-6 minutes and add tomatoes.
9. Mix well and simmer until tomatoes have softened.
10. Add the eggplants and the rest of the ingredients.
11. Cook for 5 minutes and remove from the heat.
12. Transfer everything to a large Ziploc bag.
13. Cook en sous vide for 50 minutes at 180 degrees F.
14. Serve and enjoy!

Classic New York Beef Stew

(Prep + Cook Time: 3 hours 10 minutes | Serves: 4)

NUTRITIONAL INFO PER SERVING:

Calories: 432, Protein: 37g, Carbs: 9g, Fats: 27.2g

INGREDIENTS:

1 pound New York strip steak
1 large eggplant, sliced
1 cup fire-roasted tomatoes
1 cup beef broth
½ cup burgundy
¼ cup vegetable oil
5 peppercorns, whole

2 tbsp butter, unsalted
1 bay leaf, whole
1 tbsp tomato paste
½ tbsp cayenne pepper
¼ tsp chili pepper
1 tsp salt

DIRECTIONS:

1. Rinse the meat under cold running water.
2. Pat dry with a kitchen paper and place on a clean working surface.
3. Using a sharp knife, cut into bite-sized pieces. In a large bowl, combine burgundy with oil, peppercorns, bay leaves, cayenne pepper, chili pepper, and salt.
4. Submerge meat in this mixture and refrigerate for 2 hours.
5. Remove the meat from the marinade and pat dry with a kitchen paper.
6. Reserve the liquid. Place in a large Ziploc and cook en sous vide for 2 hours at 135 degrees F for medium rare.
7. Remove from the water bath and transfer to a deep, heavy-bottomed pot. Add butter and gently melt over medium heat.
8. Add eggplant slices, tomatoes, and ¼ cup of the marinade.
9. Cook for 5 more minutes, stirring constantly.
10. Serve and enjoy!

Beef Steak with Shallots and Parsley

(Prep + Cook Time: 1 hour 15 minutes | Serves: 4)

NUTRITIONAL INFO PER SERVING:

Calories: 521, Protein: 69.3g, Carbs: 3.4g, Fats: 25g

INGREDIENTS:

1 large beefsteak, about 2 lb
2 tbsp Dijon mustard
3 tbsp olive oil
1 tbsp parsley leaves, chopped

1 tsp fresh rosemary, chopped
1 tbsp shallot, finely chopped
½ tsp dried thyme
1 garlic clove, crushed

DIRECTIONS:

1. Clean the beefsteak and cut into 1-inch thick slices. Set aside.
2. In a small bowl, combine Dijon mustard with olive oil.
3. Add parsley, rosemary, shallot, thyme, and garlic. Rub the meat with this mixture and place in a Ziploc bag.
4. Cook en sous vide for 1 hour at 136 degrees F for medium, or at 154 degrees F for well done.
5. Serve with red cabbage salad.

Sirloin Steak with Mashed Potatoes

(Prep + Cook Time: 1 hour 35 minutes | Serves: 4)

NUTRITIONAL INFO PER SERVING:

Calories: 394, Protein: 21.3g, Carbs: 35.7g, Fats: 14.8

INGREDIENTS:

4 Sirloin Steaks
2 lb of Potatoes, diced
Salt and Pepper to taste

4 tbsp Butter
Olive oil for searing

DIRECTIONS:

1. Season steaks with pepper and salt, and place in a vacuum-sealable bag. Cook en sous vide for 1 hour at 128 degrees F.
2. Place the potatoes in boiling water and cook until tender for about 20 minutes. Strain and place in a mixing bowl. Add butter and mash well. Season with pepper and salt.
3. Once the timer has stopped, remove and unseal the bag.
4. Remove the steaks from the bag and pat dry. Adjust the seasoning. Sear the steaks in a pan with oil over medium heat for about 2 minutes on each side. Serve steaks with mashed potatoes.

Beef Patties

(Prep + Cook Time: 85 minutes | Serves: 4)

NUTRITIONAL INFO PER SERVING:

Calories: 383, Protein: 37.6g, Carbs: 4.8g, Fats: 23.7g

INGREDIENTS:

1 pound lean ground beef

1 egg

2 tbsp almonds, chopped

2 tbsp flour

1 cup onions, finely chopped

2 garlic cloves, crushed

¼ cup olive oil

1 tsp salt

¼ tsp black pepper

¼ cup parsley, finely chopped

DIRECTIONS:

1. In a medium bowl, combine ground beef with onions, garlic, olive oil, salt, pepper, parsley, and almonds. Mix well with a fork and gradually add flour. Whisk in one egg and refrigerate for 40 minutes.
2. Remove the meat from the refrigerator and gently form into one-inch-thick patties, about 4-inches in diameter.
3. Place in two separate Ziploc bags and cook en sous vide for 35 minutes at 135 degrees F.

Beef Tenderloin with Baby Carrots

(Prep + Cook Time: 2 hours 10 minutes | Serves: 5

NUTRITIONAL INFO PER SERVING:
Calories: 528, Protein: 58g, Carbs: 17.4g, Fats: 24.8g

INGREDIENTS:

2 pounds Beef Tenderloin	1 tbsp butter, melted
7 baby carrots, sliced	2 tbsp fresh parsley, chopped
1 cup tomato paste	½ tsp ground black pepper
4 tbsp vegetable oil	1 tsp salt

DIRECTIONS:

1. Grease the bottom of a deep pot with oil. Wash and pat dry the meat with a kitchen paper. Using a sharp knife, cut into bite-sized pieces and season with salt. Place in the pot to brown equally for 5 minutes.
2. Now add carrots and continue to cook for 2 more minutes. Stir in tomato paste, parsley, salt, and pepper.
3. Stir in ½ cup of water.
4. Remove from the heat and transfer to a large Ziploc bag.
5. Seal the bag,, and cook en sous vide for 2 hours at 133 degrees F.

Shredded BBQ Roast

(Prep + Cook Time: 14 hours 10 minutes | Serves: 3)

NUTRITIONAL INFO PER SERVING:
Calories: 456, Protein: 35.6g, Carbs: 1g, Fats: 23.6g

INGREDIENTS:
1 medium Chuck Roast
BBQ Seasoning, of your choice
2 cups Beef Stock

DIRECTIONS:

1. Make a water bath, place the Sous Vide Cooker in it, and set to 165 degrees F. Place meat and stock in a vacuum-sealable bag, and submerge the bag in the water bath. Cook for 14 hours.
2. Once the timer has stopped, remove and unseal the bag.
3. Preheat a grill. Rub the meat with BBQ seasoning. Roast for 2 minutes on each side.
4. Remove the meat and shred it.

Red Wine Beef Ribs

(Prep + Cook Time: 6 hours 15 minutes | Serves: 3)

NUTRITIONAL INFO PER SERVING:

Calories: 453, Protein: 45.9g, Carbs: 10.3g, Fats: 23.2g

INGREDIENTS:

1 pound beef short ribs	½ cup beef stock
¼ cup red wine	¼ cup apple cider vinegar
1 tsp honey	1 garlic clove, minced
½ cup tomato paste	½ tsp salt
2 tbsp olive oil	¼ tsp black pepper, ground

DIRECTIONS:

1. Rinse and drain the ribs in a large colander.
2. Season with salt and pepper and place in a large Ziploc bag along with wine, tomato paste, beef broth, honey, and apple cider.
3. Cook en sous vide for 6 hours at 140 degrees F.
4. Remove from the water bath and set aside.
5. In a large skillet, heat the olive oil over medium-high heat. Add garlic and stir-fry until translucent.
6. Now add ribs and brown for 10 minutes.

Beef with Onions

(Prep + Cook Time: 1 hour 10 minutes | Serves: 3)

NUTRITIONAL INFO PER SERVING:

Calories: 366, Protein: 23.8g, Carbs: 10.9g, Fats: 25.6g

INGREDIENTS:

1 lb beef brisket, cut into pieces
2 large onions, chopped
¼ cup water
3 tbsp mustard

1 tsp soy sauce
1 tsp dried thyme
2 tbsp vegetable oil
2 tbsp sesame oil

DIRECTIONS:

1. Using a kitchen brush, spread the mustard over meat and sprinkle with dried thyme.
2. Place in a Ziploc bag along with soy sauce, onions, and sesame oil. Cook en sous vide for 1 hour at 154 degrees F. Remove from the water bath and set aside.
3. Heat the vegetable oil in a large skillet, over medium-high heat. Add beef and stir-fry for 5 minutes, stirring constantly. Remove from the heat and serve.

Beef Chuck Shoulder

(Prep + Cook Time: 24 hours 15 minutes | Serves: 3)

NUTRITIONAL INFO PER SERVING:

Calories: 412, Protein: 49.3g, Carbs: 9.8g, Fats: 19.2g

INGREDIENTS:

1 pound beef chuck shoulder
1 medium-sized carrot, sliced
1 large onion, chopped
¾ cup button mushrooms, sliced
1 cup beef stock

2 tbsp olive oil
4 garlic cloves, chopped
½ tsp sea salt
½ tsp black pepper, ground

DIRECTIONS:

1. Place beef chuck shoulder in a large Ziploc bag along with carrot, and half of the broth. Seal the bag and cook en sous vide for 24 hours at 140 degrees F.
2. In a large, heavy-bottomed pot, heat the olive oil and add onion and garlic. Stir-fry until translucent, for 3-4 minutes. Add beef shoulder, the remaining beef broth, 2 cups of water, mushrooms, salt, and pepper.
3. Bring it to a boil and reduce the heat to a minimum. Cook for 5 more minutes, stirring constantly.

Fire-Roasted Tomato Tenderloins

(Prep + Cook Time: 2 hours 10 minutes | Serves: 4)

NUTRITIONAL INFO PER SERVING:

Calories: 622, Protein: 61.2g, Carbs: 6.9g, Fats: 40g

INGREDIENTS:

2 lb center-cut beef tenderloin

1 cup fire-roasted tomatoes, chopped

1 tsp of salt

½ tsp ground black pepper

3 tbsp of extra virgin olive oil

2 bay leaves, whole

3 tbsp of butter, unsalted

DIRECTIONS:

1. Thoroughly rinse the meat under the running water.
2. Rub well with olive oil and season with salt and pepper.
3. Place in a large Ziploc bag along with fire-roasted tomatoes and bay leaves.
4. Seal the bag and cook en sous vide for 2 hours at 136 degrees F for medium or at 154 degrees F for well done.
5. In a large skillet, melt the butter over medium heat.
6. Place the meat in the skillet and cook for 2 minutes on each side.

Beef Pepper Meat

(Prep + Cook Time: 6 hours 5 minutes | Serves: 2)

NUTRITIONAL INFO PER SERVING:

Calories: 560, Protein: 67.1g, Carbs: 9.5g, Fats: 26.7g

INGREDIENTS:

1 pound beef Flank Steak
1 large onion finely chopped
1 tbsp butter, melted
1 tbsp parsley, finely chopped
1 tsp dried thyme, ground

1 tbsp lemon juice
1 tbsp tomato paste
½ tsp sea salt
½ tsp black pepper

DIRECTIONS:

1. Rinse the beef under cold running water. Pat dry with a kitchen paper and place on a clean working surface. Using a sharp knife, cut into bite-sized pieces.
2. Combine the ingredients in a large Ziploc bag.
3. Seal the bag and cook en sous vide for 6 hours at 138 degrees F. Remove from the water bath and open the bag. Serve immediately.

Beef Sirloin in Tomato Sauce

(Prep + Cook Time: 2 hours 5 minutes | Serves: 3)

NUTRITIONAL INFO PER SERVING:

Calories: 465, Protein: 43.2g, Carbs: 5.3g, Fats: 29.6g

INGREDIENTS:

1 pound beef sirloin medallions
1 cup fire-roasted tomatoes
1 tsp hot pepper sauce
3 garlic cloves, crushed

2 tsp chili pepper
2 tsp garlic powder
2 tsp fresh lime juice
1 tsp pink Himalayan salt

DIRECTIONS:

1. Rinse well the meat and pat dry using a kitchen paper.
2. Place in a large Ziploc bag.
3. In a medium-sized bowl, combine the fire roasted tomatoes with hot pepper sauce, crushed garlic, chili pepper, garlic powder, lime juice, and salt.
4. Add the mixture to the bag and seal it.
5. Cook en sous vide for 2 hours at 135 degrees F.

Stuffed Collard Greens

(Prep + Cook Time: 50 minutes | Serves: 3)

NUTRITIONAL INFO PER SERVING:

Calories: 180, Protein: 8.3g, Carbs: 10.5g, Fats: 12.3g

INGREDIENTS:

1 pound collard greens, steamed
1 pound lean ground beef
1 small onion, finely chopped
1 tbsp olive oil
½ tsp salt
¼ tsp black pepper
1 tsp fresh mint, finely chopped

DIRECTIONS:

1. Boil a large pot of water and add the greens. Briefly cook, for 2-3 minutes. Drain and gently squeeze the greens and set aside.
2. In a large bowl, combine ground beef, onion, oil, salt, pepper, and mint. Stir well until incorporated.
3. Place leaves on your work surface, vein side up. Use one tablespoon of the meat mixture and place it in the bottom center of each leaf. Fold the sides over and roll up tightly.
4. Tuck in the sides and gently transfer to a large Ziploc bag.
5. Seal the bag and cook en sous vide for 40 minutes at 135 degrees F. Serve cold.

Portobello Veal

(Prep + Cook Time: 3 hours 5 minutes | Serves: 4)

NUTRITIONAL INFO PER SERVING:

Calories: 406, Protein: 56.7g, Carbs: 2g, Fats: 17.4g

INGREDIENTS:

2 pounds veal cutlets

1 cup beef stock

4 Portobello mushrooms

1 tsp garlic powder

1 tbsp oregano, dried

3 tbsp balsamic vinegar

1 tsp pink Himalayan salt

DIRECTIONS:

1. In a medium-sized bowl, combine the beef stock with garlic powder, oregano, balsamic vinegar, and salt.
2. Rub well each cutlet with this mixture and place in a large Ziploc bag.
3. Wash and slice mushrooms lengthwise.
4. Add to Ziploc bag along with the remaining marinade. Seal the bag.
5. Cook en sous vide for 3 hours at 140 degrees F.

Beef and Ginger Patties

(Prep + Cook Time: 1 hour 25 minutes | Serves: 3)

NUTRITIONAL INFO PER SERVING:

Calories: 426, Protein: 46.8g, Carbs: 5.5g, Fats: 23.7g

INGREDIENTS:

1 pound ground beef

1 cup onions, finely chopped

3 tbsp olive oil

¼ cup fresh cilantro, chopped

¼ cup fresh mint, chopped

2 tsp ginger paste

1 tsp cayenne pepper

2 tsp salt

DIRECTIONS:

1. In a large bowl, combine ground beef with onions, olive oil, cilantro, mint, coriander, ginger paste, cayenne pepper, and salt.
2. Use about one cup of the mixture to mold patties and refrigerate for 15 minutes.
3. Remove from the refrigerator and transfer to separate Ziploc bags.
4. Cook en sous vide for 1 hour at 130 degrees F.
5. Preheat a large, non-stick grill pan and brown patties for 2 minutes on each side.

Garlic Burgers

(Prep + Cook Time: 45 minutes | Serves: 4)

NUTRITIONAL INFO PER SERVING:

Calories: 407, Protein: 42.2g, Carbs: 10.6g, Fats: 21.2g

INGREDIENTS:

1 pound lean ground beef

3 garlic cloves, crushed

2 tbsp breadcrumbs

3 eggs, beaten

¼ cup lentils, soaked

¼ cup oil, divided in half

1 tbsp cilantro, finely chopped

DIRECTIONS:

1. In a medium-sized bowl, combine lentils with beef, garlic, cilantro, breadcrumbs, eggs, and three tablespoons of oil.
2. Using your hands, shape burgers and place on a lightly floured working surface.
3. Gently place each burger in a Ziploc bag and seal.
4. Cook en sous vide for 35 minutes, at 134 degrees F. Remove from the bag and set aside.
5. Heat the remaining oil in a large skillet. Brown burgers for 2-3 minutes on each side for extra crispiness.

Lime and Garlic Pork Tenderloin

(Prep + Cook Time: 2 hours 10 minutes | Serves: 2)

NUTRITIONAL INFO PER SERVING:

Calories: 185, Protein: 31.5g, Carbs: 3g, Fats: 5.4g,

INGREDIENTS:

2 tbsp Garlic Powder

2 tbsp Ground Cumin

2 tbsp Dried Thyme

2 tbsp Dried Rosemary

1 pinch Lime Sea Salt

2 Pork Tenderloins, silver skin removed

2 tbsp Olive Oil

2 tbsp Salt

3 tbsp Unsalted Butter

DIRECTIONS:

1. Make a water bath, place Sous Vide cooker in it, and set to 140 degrees F.
2. Add the cumin, garlic powder, thyme, lime salt, rosemary, and lime salt to a bowl and mix evenly.
3. Brush the pork with olive oil, rub it with salt and cumin herb mixture.
4. Put the pork into two separate vacuum-sealable bags. Release air by the water displacement method and seal the bags.
5. Submerge in the water bath and set the timer for 2 hours.
6. Once the timer has stopped, unseal the bags. Remove the pork and pat dry using a napkin.
7. Preheat a cast iron pan over high heat and add the butter. Add the pork and sear to golden brown, about 2 minutes per side.
8. Let the pork rest on a cutting board.
9. Cut into 2-inch medallions and serve.

Pork Ribs with Coconut-Peanut Sauce

(Prep + Cook Time: 10 hours 33 minutes | Serves: 3)

NUTRITIONAL INFO PER SERVING:

Calories: 495, Protein: 36.2g, Carbs: 12g, Fats: 27.4g

INGREDIENTS:

½ cup Coconut Milk,

2 ½ tbsp Peanut Butter

2 tbsp Soy Sauce

1 tbsp Sugar

3 inches Fresh Lemongrass

1 ½ tbsp Pepper Sauce

1 ½ inch Ginger, peeled

3 cloves Garlic

2 ½ tsp Sesame Oil

13 oz Boneless Pork Ribs

DIRECTIONS:

1. Prepare a water bath and place a Sous Vide machine in it. Set the Sous Vide Machine to 135 degrees F.
2. Blend all the listed ingredients in a blender except the pork ribs and cilantro until it's a smooth paste.
3. Place the ribs in a vacuum-sealable bag and add the blended sauce.
4. Release air by the water displacement method and seal the bag. Place the bag in the water bath and set the timer for 10 hours.
5. Once the timer has stopped, take the bag out, unseal it and remove the ribs. Transfer to a plate and keep warm.
6. Put a skillet over medium heat and pour in the sauce from the bag. Bring to a boil for 5 minutes, reduce the heat, and simmer for 12 minutes.
7. Add the ribs and coat with the sauce. Simmer for 6 minutes.
8. Serve with steamed greens.

Pork Chops with Mushroom Sauce

(Prep + Cook Time: 1 hour 45 minutes | Serves: 3)

NUTRITIONAL INFO PER SERVING:

Calories: 297, Protein: 25.7g Carbs: 11g, Fats: 18g

INGREDIENTS:

3 Pork Chops

Black Pepper Powder to taste

3 tbsp Butter, unsalted

6 oz Mushrooms

½ cup Beef Stock

2 tbsp Worcestershire Sauce

3 tbsp Garlic Chives, chopped

DIRECTIONS:

1. Make a water bath, place a Sous Vide cooker in it, and set to 140 degrees F. Rub pork chops with salt and pepper and put them in a vacuum-sealable bag. Submerge the bag in the water bath. Set the timer for 90 minutes.
2. Once the timer has stopped, unseal the bag. Remove the pork and pat it dry using a napkin. Discard the juices.
3. Place a skillet over medium heat and melt 1 tablespoon butter. Sear the pork for 5 minutes on both sides. Set aside.
4. With the skillet still over the heat, add the remaining butter and mushrooms and cook for 10 minutes. Turn heat off. Season with pepper and salt.
5. Serve pork chops with mushroom sauce.

Jerk Pork Ribs

(Prep + Cook Time: 20 hours 10 minutes | Serves: 6)

NUTRITIONAL INFO PER SERVING:

Calories: 380, Protein: 21.2g Carbs: 4g, Fats: 21.5g

INGREDIENTS:

5 lb Baby Back Pork Ribs,

½ cup Jerk Seasoning Mix

DIRECTIONS:

1. Cut the racks into halves and season with half of the jerk seasoning. Place in 4 separate vacuum-sealable bags. Cook for 20 hours at 145 degrees F.
2. Once the timer has stopped, remove and unseal the bags.
3. Transfer the ribs to a foiled baking sheet and preheat a broiler to high.
4. Rub the ribs with the remaining jerk seasoning and place in the broiler. Broil for 5 minutes. Slice into single ribs.

BBQ Pork Ribs

(Prep + Cook Time: 1 hour 10 minutes | Serves: 4)

NUTRITIONAL INFO PER SERVING:

Calories: 290, Protein: 14g, Carbs: 14g, Fats: 17g

INGREDIENTS:

1 lb Pork Ribs   1 tsp Salt
1 tsp Garlic Powder   1 cup BBQ Sauce
1 tsp Black Pepper Powder

DIRECTIONS:

1. Rub salt and pepper graciously on the pork ribs.
2. Place the ribs in a vacuum-sealable bag, release air and seal. Put in the water and cook for 1 hour at 140 degrees F.
3. Once the timer has stopped, remove and unseal the bag.
4. Remove ribs and coat with BBQ sauce. Place aside.
5. Preheat a grill.
6. Once it is hot, sear the ribs all around for 5 minutes.
7. Serve with a dip of choice.

Herb Crusted Lamb Rack

(Prep + Cook Time: 2 hours | Serves: 6

NUTRITIONAL INFO PER SERVING:

Calories: 250, Protein: 14g, Carbs: 4g, Fats: 20g

INGREDIENTS:

Lamb Rack:

3 large Racks of Lamb
Salt to taste
3 tsp Black Pepper Powder

1 sprig Rosemary
2 tbsp Olive Oil

Herb Crust:

2 tbsp Fresh Rosemary Leaves
½ cup Macadamia Nuts
2 tbsp Dijon Mustard
½ cup Fresh Parsley

2 tbsp Fresh Thyme Leaves
2 tbsp Lemon Zest
2 cloves Garlic
2 Egg Whites

DIRECTIONS:

1. Make a water bath, place the Sous Vide Cooker in it, and set to 140 degrees F.
2. Pat dry the lamb with a napkin and rub the meat with salt and black pepper.
3. Place a pan over medium heat and add olive oil. Sear the lamb on both sides for 8 minutes. Remove and set aside. Add garlic and rosemary to the pan, toast for 1 minute and pour over the lamb. Remove the lamb to a plate and leave cool for 5 minutes.
4. Place lamb, garlic, and rosemary in a vacuum-sealable bag, release air by the water displacement method and seal the bag. Submerge the bag in the water bath. Cook for 1 hour 30 minutes.
5. Once the timer has stopped, remove the bag, unseal and take out the lamb. Whisk the egg whites and place aside.
6. Blend the remaining listed herb crust ingredients using a blender and place aside.

7. Pat dry the lamb using a napkin and brush the meat with the egg whites.
8. Dip into the herb mixture and coat graciously.
9. Place the lamb racks with crust side up on a baking sheet. Bake in an oven for 15 minutes.
10. Gently slice each cutlet.
11. Serve with pureed vegetables.

Roasted Pork Neck

(Prep + Cook Time: 1 hour 20 minutes | Serves: 5)

NUTRITIONAL INFO PER SERVING:
Calories: 315, Protein: 28.7g, Carbs: 6g, Fats: 20.8g

INGREDIENTS:

2 lb Pork Neck, boneless, sliced

4 tbsp Olive Oil

2 tsp Soy Sauce

2 tbsp Barbecue Sauce

2 tbsp Sugar

4 sprigs Rosemary

4 sprigs Thyme

2 cloves Garlic, minced

¼ tsp Salt

¼ tsp White Pepper Powder

¼ tsp Red Pepper Flakes

DIRECTIONS:

1. Rub salt and pepper graciously on the pork.
2. Place the meat in 2 separate vacuum-sealable bags, release air and seal them.
3. Put in the water bath and cook for 1 hour at 140 degrees F.
4. Once the timer has stopped, remove and unseal the bags. Mix the remaining listed ingredients.
5. Preheat oven to 425 degrees F.
6. Put the pork on a roasting pan and rub soy sauce mixture generously into the pork. Roast in the oven for 15 minutes.
7. Let pork cool before slicing.
8. Serve with steamed greens.

Goat Cheese Lamb Ribs

(Prep + Cook Time: 4 hours 5 minutes | Serves: 2)

NUTRITIONAL INFO PER SERVING:

Calories: 165, Protein: 10.1g, Carbs: 8g, Fats: 13.5g

INGREDIENTS:

Ribs:

2 half racks Lamb Ribs

2 tbsp Vegetable Oil

1 clove Garlic, minced

2 tbsp Rosemary, chopped

1 tbsp Fennel Pollen

½ tsp Black Pepper Powder

½ tsp Cayenne Pepper

Salt to taste

To Garnish:

8 oz Goat Cheese, crumbled

2 oz Roasted Walnuts, chopped

3 tbsp Parsley, chopped

DIRECTIONS:

1. Make a water bath, place the Sous Vide Cooker in it, and set to 134 degrees F.
2. Mix the listed lamb ingredients except for the lamb.
3. Pat dry the lamb using a napkin and rub the meat with the spice mixture.
4. Place the meat in a vacuum-sealable bag, release air by the water displacement method, seal and submerge in the water bath. Set the timer for 4 hours.
5. Once the timer has stopped, remove the bag and remove the lamb.
6. Oil and preheat a grill on high heat. Place the lamb on it and sear to become golden brown. Cut the ribs between the bones.
7. Garnish with goat cheese, walnuts and parsley. Serve with a hot sauce dip.

Lamb Chops with Basil Chimichurri

(Prep + Cook Time: 3 hours 40 minutes | Serves: 6)

NUTRITIONAL INFO PER SERVING:

Calories: 226, Protein: 15.8g, Carbs: 7g, Fats: 17.5g,

INGREDIENTS:

Lamb Chops:

3 Lamb Racks, frenched	⅓ tsp Salt
3 cloves Garlic, crushed	1 tsp Black Pepper Powder

Basil Chimichurri:

1 ½ cups Fresh Basil, chopped	½ cup Olive Oil
2 Banana Shallots, diced	3 tbsp Red Wine Vinegar
3 cloves Garlic, minced	½ tsp Salt
1 tsp Red Pepper Flakes	½ tsp Black Pepper

DIRECTIONS:

1. Prepare a water bath and place the Sous Vide Cooker in it.
2. Set the Sous Vide Cooker to 140 degrees F.
3. Pat dry the racks with a napkin and rub with pepper and salt.
4. Place meat and garlic in a vacuum-sealable bag, release air by water displacement method and seal the bag.
5. Submerge the bag in the water bath. Cook for 2 hours.
6. Make the basil chimichurri: mix all the listed ingredients in a bowl.
7. Cover with cling film and refrigerate for 1 hour 30 minutes.
8. Once the Sous Vide timer has stopped, remove the bag and open it. Remove the lamb and pat dry using a napkin.
9. Sear with a torch to golden brown, about 5 minutes. Spread the basil chimichurri over the lamb.
10. Serve with a side of steamed greens.

Spicy Lamb Roast

(Prep + Cook Time: 8 hours 16 minutes | Serves: 6)

NUTRITIONAL INFO PER SERVING:

Calories: 375, Protein: 33.3g, Carbs: 4g, Fats: 12.5g

INGREDIENTS:

1 ½ tbsp Canola Oil

1 tbsp Black Mustard Seeds

1 tsp Cumin Seeds

Salt to taste

Black Pepper to taste

4 lb Butterflied Lamb Leg

½ cup Mint Leaves, chopped

½ cup Cilantro Leaves, chopped

1 Shallot, minced

1 clove Garlic, minced

2 Red Jalapenos, minced

1 tbsp Red Wine Vinegar

1 ½ tbsp Olive Oil

DIRECTIONS:

1. Place a skillet over medium heat on a stove top.
2. Add ½ tablespoon of olive oil; once it has heated add cumin and mustard seeds and cook for 1 minute.
3. Turn off heat and transfer seeds to a bowl.
4. Mix in salt and black pepper.
5. Spread the spice mixture inside the lamb leg and roll it. Secure with a butcher's twine at 1- inch intervals.
6. Season with salt and pepper and massage.
7. Make a water bath and place the Sous Vide Cooker in it.
8. Set the Sous Vide cooker to 140 degrees F.
9. Place the lamb leg in a vacuum-sealable bag, release air by the water displacement method, seal and submerge in the water bath. Cook for 8 hours.
10. Make the sauce; add to the cumin mustard mixture, shallot, cilantro, garlic, red wine vinegar, mint, and red chili.
11. Mix and season with salt and pepper. Place aside.
12. Once the Sous Vide timer has stopped, remove and unseal the bag.
13. Remove the lamb and pat dry using a napkin.

14. Add canola oil to cast iron over high heat, and sear lamb for 10 minutes on both sides until brown.
15. Remove twine and slice lamb. Serve with sauce.

Balsamic Pork Chops

(Prep + Cook Time: 1 hour 10 minutes | Serves: 5

NUTRITIONAL INFO PER SERVING:

Calories: 658, Protein: 40.9g, Carbs: 0.8g, Fats: 53.5g

INGREDIENTS:

2 pounds pork chops

3 garlic cloves, crushed

½ tsp dried basil

½ tsp dried thyme

¼ cup balsamic vinegar

1 tsp pink Himalayan salt

3 tbsp extra virgin olive oil

DIRECTIONS:

1. Rinse the meat and pat dry with a kitchen paper.
2. Sprinkle with salt and set aside.
3. In a small bowl, combine vinegar with olive oil, thyme, basil, and garlic.
4. Stir well and spread the mixture evenly over meat.
5. Place in a large Ziploc bag and seal it.
6. Cook en sous vide for 1 hour at 144 degrees F for medium rare or at 158 degrees F for well done.

Lamb Shoulder

(Prep + Cook Time: 8 hours 14 minutes | Serves: 3)

NUTRITIONAL INFO PER SERVING:

Calories: 455, Protein: 31.4g, Carbs: 2g, Fats: 27.8

INGREDIENTS:

1 lb. Lamb Shoulder, deboned

1 tsp Salt

2 tsp Black Pepper

2 tbsp Olive Oil

1 Garlic Clove, crushed

1 sprig Thyme

1 sprig Rosemary

DIRECTIONS:

1. Prepare a water bath and place the Sous Vide Cooker in it.
2. Set the Sous Vide Cooker to 145 deh¡grees F. Pat dry the lamb shoulders using a napkin and rub with pepper and salt.
3. Place the lamb and the remaining listed ingredients in a vacuum-sealable bag.
4. Release air by the water displacement method, seal and submerge the bag in the water bath. Set the timer to 8 hours.
5. Once the timer has stopped, remove the bag and transfer the lamb shoulders to baking dish. Strain the juices into a saucepan and cook over medium heat for 2 minutes.
6. Preheat a grill for and grill the shoulder until golden brown and crispy, about 10 minutes.
7. Serve the lamb shoulder and sauce with buttered greens.

Spicy Meatballs

(Prep + Cook Time: 60 minutes | Serves: 3)

NUTRITIONAL INFO PER SERVING:

Calories: 356, Protein: 47.5g, Carbs: 3.7g, Fats: 16.1g

INGREDIENTS:

1 pound lean ground beef

2 tbsp all-purpose flour

¼ cup milk

½ tsp ground black pepper

¼ tsp chili pepper

3 garlic cloves, crushed

1 tsp salt

½ cup celery leaves, chopped

DIRECTIONS:

1. In a large bowl, combine ground beef with flour, milk, black pepper, chili pepper, garlic, salt, and celery. Shape bite-sized balls and in a large Ziploc bag.
2. Seal the bag and cook for 55 minutes at 136 degrees F.

Garlic Pork Fillets

(Prep + Cook Time: 2 hours 5 minutes | Serves: 3)

NUTRITIONAL INFO PER SERVING:

Calories: 240, Protein: 44g, Carbs: 1.9g, Fats: 19.7g

INGREDIENTS:

1 pound pork fillets

1 cup vegetable broth

2 garlic cloves, minced

1 tsp garlic powder

½ tsp ground black pepper

DIRECTIONS:

1. Rub the meat with garlic powder. Place in a Ziploc bag along with broth, minced garlic, garlic powder, and pepper.
2. Seal the bag and cook en sous vide for 2 hours at 136 degrees F.

Veal Chops with Pine Mushrooms

(Prep + Cook Time: 3 hours 20 minutes | Serves: 5

NUTRITIONAL INFO PER SERVING:

Calories: 301, Protein: 25.1g, Carbs: 3.5g, Fats: 21g

INGREDIENTS:

1 pound veal chops

1 pound pine mushrooms

½ cup lemon juice

1 tbsp bay leaves, crushed

5 peppercorns

3 tbsp vegetable oil

2 tbsp extra virgin olive oil

1 tsp salt, divided in half

DIRECTIONS:

1. Season the meat with salt. Place in a Ziploc bag along with lemon juice, bay leaves, peppercorns, and vegetable oil. Seal the bag. Cook for 3 hours at 135 degrees F.
2. Remove from the water bath and set aside.
3. Heat the olive oil in a large skillet.
4. Add pine mushrooms and stir-fry over medium heat until all the liquid evaporates, about 10 minutes.
5. Now add veal chops along with its marinade and continue to cook for 3 more minutes per side.

Rosemary Meatballs with Yogurt

(Prep + Cook Time: 1 hour 5 minutes | Serves: 3)

NUTRITIONAL INFO PER SERVING:

Calories: 471, Protein: 49.3g, Carbs: 9.8g, Fats: 25.4g

INGREDIENTS:

1 pound lean ground beef

3 garlic cloves, crushed

¼ cup all-purpose flour

1 large egg, beaten

1 cup Greek yogurt

1 tbsp rosemary, crushed

½ tsp sea salt

3 tbsp extra-virgin olive oil

DIRECTIONS:

1. Place the meat in a large bowl.
2. Add crushed garlic, flour, egg, fresh rosemary, salt, and oil.
3. Combine the ingredients together.
4. Using your hands, shape bite-sized balls and place them in a large Ziploc bag.
5. Seal the bag and cook in a water bath for 1 hour at 136 degrees F.
6. Remove from the bath and top with Greek yogurt to serve.

Stuffed Bell Peppers

(Prep + Cook Time: 2 hours 30 minutes | Serves: 6)

NUTRITIONAL INFO PER SERVING:

Calories: 250, Protein: 24.5g, Carbs: 11.6g, Fats: 12.1g

INGREDIENTS:

6 medium-sized bell peppers
1 pound lean ground beef
1 onion, finely chopped
1 tomato, chopped

½ tsp cayenne pepper, ground
3 tbsp extra-virgin olive oil
½ tsp salt
¼ tsp black pepper, ground

DIRECTIONS:

1. Cut the stem end of each pepper and remove the seeds.
2. Rinse and set aside.
3. In a large bowl, combine ground beef, onion, tomato, cayenne pepper, olive oil, salt, and pepper.
4. Use two tablespoons of the mixture to fill each bell pepper.
5. Gently place in a large Ziploc bag and cook en sous vide for 2 hours at 140 degrees F.
6. Remove the peppers from the bag and chill for about 30 minutes before serving.

Wild Salmon Steaks

(Prep + Cook Time: 55 minutes | Serves: 4)

NUTRITIONAL INFO PER SERVING:

Calories: 324, Protein: 39.7g, Carbs: 29.3g, Fats: 5.2g

INGREDIENTS:

2 pounds wild salmon steaks
3 garlic cloves, crushed
1 tbsp fresh rosemary, chopped
1 tbsp lemon juice
1 tbsp orange juice
1 tsp orange zest
1 tsp pink Himalayan salt
1 cup fish stock

DIRECTIONS:

1. Combine orange juice with lemon juice, rosemary, garlic, orange zest, and salt. Brush the mixture over each steak and refrigerate for 20 minutes.
2. Transfer to a Ziploc bag and add fish stock. Seal the bag and cook en sous vide for 45 minutes at 131 degrees F.
3. Preheat a large, non-stick grill pan. Remove the steaks from Ziploc and grill for 3 minutes on each side, until lightly charred.

Marinated Catfish Fillets

(Prep + Cook Time: 80 minutes | Serves: 3)

NUTRITIONAL INFO PER SERVING:

Calories: 368, Protein: 25.1g, Carbs: 8.7g, Fats: 26.3g

INGREDIENTS:

1 pound catfish fillet
½ cup lemon juice
½ cup parsley, chopped
2 garlic cloves, crushed
1 cup onions, finely chopped
1 tbsp fresh dill, chopped
1 tbsp rosemary, chopped
2 cups apple juice
2 tbsp Dijon mustard
1 cup extra virgin olive oil

DIRECTIONS:

1. In a large bowl, combine lemon juice, parsley leaves, crushed garlic, finely chopped onions, fresh dill, rosemary, apple juice, mustard, and olive oil. Whisk together until well incorporated.
2. Submerge fillets in this mixture and cover with a tight lid. Refrigerate for 30 minutes.
3. Remove from the refrigerator and place in 2 separate Ziploc bags. Seal the bags, and cook en sous vide for 40 minutes at 129 degrees F.
4. Remove from the bags and drain but make sure to reserve the liquid.
5. Transfer to a serving platter and drizzle with its liquid.

Cilantro Trout

(Prep + Cook Time: 1 hour | Serves: 4)

NUTRITIONAL INFO PER SERVING:

Calories: 567, Protein: 57.9g, Carbs: 2.8g, Fats: 33.6g

INGREDIENTS:

2 pounds trout, 4 pieces

5 garlic cloves

1 tbsp sea salt

4 tbsp olive oil

1 cup cilantro leaves, chopped

2 tbsp rosemary, chopped

¼ cup lemon juice

DIRECTIONS:

1. Rub the fish with salt.
2. Combine garlic with olive oil, cilantro, rosemary, and lemon juice. Use the mixture to fill each fish.
3. Place in a Ziploc bag and seal.
4. Cook en sous vide for 55 minutes at 120 degrees F.

Sous Vide Halibut

(Prep + Cook Time: 70 minutes | Serves: 4)

NUTRITIONAL INFO PER SERVING:

Calories: 377, Protein: 53g, Carbs: 2.1g, Fats: 16.4g

INGREDIENTS:

1 pound halibut fillets

3 tbsp olive oil

¼ cup of shallots, finely chopped

1 tsp freshly grated lemon zest

½ tsp dried thyme, ground

1 tbsp fresh parsley, chopped

1 tsp fresh dill, finely chopped

½ tsp sea salt

¼ tsp ground black pepper

DIRECTIONS:

1. Wash the fish under cold running water and pat dry with a kitchen paper. Cut into thin slices generously sprinkle with salt and pepper.
2. Place in a large Ziploc bag and add two tablespoons of olive oil. Season with shallots, thyme, parsley, dill, salt, and pepper.
3. Press the bag to remove the air and seal. Shake the bag to coat all the fillets with spices and refrigerate for 30 minutes before cooking.
4. Cook en sous vide for 35 minutes at 136 degrees F.
5. Remove the bag from the water and set aside to cool for a while. Now, place it on a kitchen paper and drain. Remove the herbs.
6. Preheat the remaining oil in a large skillet over medium-high temperature. Add fillets and cook for 2 minutes. Flip the fillets and cook for about 35-40 seconds and then remove from the heat.
7. Transfer the fish again to a paper towel and remove the excessive fat.
8. Serve immediately.

Herb-Marinated Tuna Steaks

(Prep + Cook Time: 80 minutes | Serves: 5

NUTRITIONAL INFO PER SERVING:

Calories: 521, Protein: 57.2g, Carbs: 5.5g, Fats: 29.8g

INGREDIENTS:

2 pounds tuna steaks, about 1-inch thick

1 tsp dried thyme, ground

1 tsp fresh basil, finely chopped

¼ cup finely chopped shallots

2 tbsp fresh parsley, chopped

1 tbsp fresh dill, finely chopped

1 tsp freshly grated lemon zest

½ cup sesame seeds

4 tbsp olive oil

1 tsp sea salt

¼ tsp ground black pepper

DIRECTIONS:

1. Wash the tuna fillets under cold running water and pat dry with a kitchen paper. Set aside.
2. In a large bowl, combine thyme, basil, shallots, parsley, dill, oil, salt, and pepper.
3. Mix until well incorporated and then soak the steaks in this marinade. Coat well and refrigerate for 30 minutes before cooking.
4. Place the steaks in a large Ziploc bag along with marinade.
5. Press the bag to remove the air and seal.
6. Cook en sous vide for 40 minutes at 105 degrees F.
7. Remove the steaks from the bag and transfer to a kitchen paper. Gently pat dry and remove the herbs.
8. Preheat a large non-stick skillet over medium-high temperature.
9. Roll the steaks in sesame seeds and transfer to the skillet. Cook for 1 minute on each side and remove from the heat.

Chili Smelts

(Prep + Cook Time: 70 minutes | Serves: 5

NUTRITIONAL INFO PER SERVING:

Calories: 471, Protein: 21.1g, Carbs: 2.2g, Fats: 43.4g

INGREDIENTS:

1 pound fresh smelts
½ cup lemon juice
3 garlic cloves, crushed
1 tsp salt

1 cup extra virgin olive oil
2 tbsp fresh dill, chopped
1 tbsp chives, minced
1 tbsp chili pepper, ground

DIRECTIONS:

1. Rinse smelts under cold running water and drain. Set aside.
2. In a large bowl, combine olive oil with lemon juice, crushed garlic, sea salt, finely chopped dill, minced chives, and chili pepper.
3. Place smelts into this mixture and cover.
4. Refrigerate for 20 minutes.
5. Remove from the refrigerator and place in a large Ziploc bag along with the marinade.
6. Cook en sous vide for 40 minutes at 104 degrees F.
7. Remove from the water bath and drain but reserve the liquid.
8. Preheat a large, non-stick skillet, over medium-high heat.
9. Add smelts and briefly cook, for 3-4 minutes, turning them over.
10. Remove from the heat and transfer to a serving plate.
11. Drizzle with its marinade and serve immediately.

Salmon & Kale Salad with Avocado

(Prep + Cook Time: 45 minutes | Serves: 3)

NUTRITIONAL INFO PER SERVING:

Calories: 298, Protein: 30.4g, Carbs: 12.6g, Fats: 15.1g

INGREDIENTS:

1 pound skinless salmon fillet

½ tsp salt

¼ tsp black pepper

½ organic lemon, juiced

1 tbsp olive oil

1 cup kale leaves, shredded

½ cup roasted carrots, sliced

½ ripe avocado, cubed

1 tbsp fresh dill

1 tbsp fresh parsley leaves

DIRECTIONS :

1. Season the fillet with salt and pepper on both sides and place in a large Ziploc bag.
2. Seal the bag, and cook en sous vide for 40 minutes at 130 degrees F.
3. Remove the salmon from a water bath and set aside to cool.
4. Whisk together the lemon juice, a pinch of salt and black pepper in a mixing bowl and gradually add in olive oil while whisking constantly.
5. Add the shredded kale and toss to evenly coat with vinaigrette.
6. Add in the roasted carrots, avocados, dill, and parsley. Gently toss to combine.
7. Transfer to a serving bowl and serve with salmon on top.

Tilapia Stew

(Prep + Cook Time: 65 minutes | Serves: 3)

NUTRITIONAL INFO PER SERVING:

Calories: 314, Protein: 30g, Carbs: 15.9g, Fats: 15.8g

INGREDIENTS:

1 pound tilapia fillets
½ cup onions, finely chopped
1 cup carrots, finely chopped
½ cup cilantro, chopped
3 garlic cloves, chopped
1 cup bell peppers, chopped

1 tsp Italian seasoning mix
1 tsp cayenne pepper
1 cup fresh tomato juice
1 tsp salt
½ tsp black pepper
3 tbsp olive oil

DIRECTIONS:

1. Heat the olive oil over medium-high heat. Add chopped onions and stir-fry until translucent, about 3 minutes.
2. Now add bell pepper, carrots, garlic, cilantro, Italian seasoning mix, cayenne pepper, salt, and black pepper. Give it a good stir and cook for 10 more minutes.
3. Remove from the heat and transfer to a large Ziploc bag along with tomato juice and tilapia fillets. Cook en sous vide for 50 minutes at 135 degrees F. Remove from the water bath and serve.

Salmon with Asparagus

(Prep + Cook Time: 40 minutes | Serves: 5

NUTRITIONAL INFO PER SERVING:

Calories: 543, Protein: 39.6g, Carbs: 2.8g, Fats: 40.6g

INGREDIENTS:

1 pound wild salmon fillet
1 tbsp olive oil

1 tbsp dried oregano
12 medium asparagus spears

| 4 white onion rings | ½ tsp salt |
| 1 tbsp fresh parsley | ¼ tsp pepper |

DIRECTIONS:

1. Season the fillet with oregano, salt, and pepper on both sides and lightly brush with olive oil.
2. Place in a large Ziploc along with other ingredients. Combine all spices in a mixing bowl.
3. Rub the mixture evenly on both sides of the steak and place in a large Ziploc bag.
4. Seal the bag, and cook en sous vide for 35 minutes at 134 degrees F.

Basil Cod with Mushrooms

(Prep + Cook Time: 55 minutes | Serves: 4)

NUTRITIONAL INFO PER SERVING:

Calories: 387, Protein: 33.6g, Carbs: 12.2g, Fats: 22.9g

INGREDIENTS:

1 pound cod fillet	1 medium-sized carrot, sliced
1 cup fire-roasted tomatoes	¼ cup olive oil
1 tbsp basil, dried	1 medium-sized onion, finely chopped
1 cup fish stock	
2 tbsp tomato paste	2 garlic cloves, crushed
3 celery stalks, finely chopped	½ cup button mushrooms

DIRECTIONS:

1. Heat the olive oil in a large skillet, over medium heat.
2. Add chopped celery stalks, onions, and carrots. Stir-fry for 10 minutes.
3. Remove from the heat and transfer to a Ziploc bag along with other ingredients.
4. Cook en sous vide for 40 minutes at 122 degrees F.

Sea Bass in White Wine

(Prep + Cook Time: 1 hour 50 minutes | Serves: 2)

NUTRITIONAL INFO PER SERVING:

Calories: 620, Protein: 61g, Carbs: 2.6g, Fats: 39.7g

INGREDIENTS:

1 pound sea bass, cleaned
1 cup of extra virgin olive oil
1 lemon, juiced
1 tbsp sweetener
1 tbsp dried rosemary

½ tbsp dried oregano
2 garlic cloves, crushed
½ cup white wine
1 tsp sea salt

DIRECTIONS:

1. Combine olive oil with lemon juice, sweetener, rosemary, oregano, crushed garlic, wine, and salt in a large bowl. Submerge fish in this mixture and marinate for 1 hour in the refrigerator.
2. Remove from the refrigerator and drain but reserve the liquid for serving.
3. Place fillets in a large Ziploc bag and seal. Cook en sous vide for 40 minutes at 130 degrees F.
4. Drizzle the remaining marinade over fillets and serve.

Sardines en Sous Vide

(Prep + Cook Time: 1 hour 5 minutes | Serves: 3)

NUTRITIONAL INFO PER SERVING:

Calories: 471, Protein: 49.3g, Carbs: 9.8g, Fats: 25.4g

INGREDIENTS:

2 pounds sardines
¼ cup extra-virgin olive oil
3 garlic cloves, crushed
1 tsp dried rosemary, chopped

1 large lemon, freshly juiced
2 sprigs fresh mint
Sea salt and pepper, to taste

DIRECTIONS:

1. Wash and clean each fish but keep the skin. Pat dry using a kitchen paper.
2. In a large bowl, combine olive oil with garlic, rosemary, lemon juice, fresh mint, salt, and pepper.
3. Place the sardines in a large Ziploc bag along with the marinade.
4. Cook in a water bath for 1 hour at 104 degrees F.
5. Remove from the bath and drain but reserve the sauce.
6. Drizzle fish with sauce and steamed leek. Enjoy!

Rosemary Scallops

(Prep + Cook Time: 40 minutes | Serves: 3)

NUTRITIONAL INFO PER SERVING:

Calories: 436, Protein: 23.9g, Carbs: 6.5g, Fats: 35.8g

INGREDIENTS:

1 pound fresh Scallops, whole
½ cup extra virgin olive oil
1 tbsp of pink Himalayan salt

1 tbsp of dried rosemary
3 garlic cloves, crushed
3 cherry tomatoes, halved

DIRECTIONS:

1. In a large bowl, combine olive oil with salt, dried rosemary, cherry tomatoes, and crushed garlic.
2. Submerge scallops in this mixture and transfer to refrigerator for one hour.
3. Remove from the refrigerator and drain.
4. Place scallops and cherry tomatoes in a large Ziploc bag.
5. Cook en sous vide for 35 minutes at 126 degrees F.
6. Enjoy!

White Wine Mussels

(Prep + Cook Time: 1 hour 15 minutes | Serves: 3)

NUTRITIONAL INFO PER SERVING:

Calories: 341, Protein: 18.9g, Carbs: 13.5g, Fats: 17.7g

INGREDIENTS:

1 pound fresh mussels

3 tbsp extra virgin olive oil

1 cup onions, finely chopped

¼ cup fresh parsley, chopped

3 tbsp fresh thyme, chopped

1 tbsp lemon zest

1 cup dry white wine

DIRECTIONS:

1. Toss the mussels in a large bowl filled with cold water.
2. Let it stand for 30 minutes. Remove from the water and drain in a large colander. Set aside.
3. In a medium-sized skillet, heat the oil. Add onions and stir-fry until translucent, about 3 minutes.
4. Add lemon zest, parsley, and thyme. Give it a good stir and transfer to a Ziploc bag. Add mussels and one cup of dry white wine.
5. Seal the bag, and cook en sous vide for 40 minutes at 104 degrees F.

Fried Lemon Shrimp

(Prep + Cook Time: 40 minutes | Serves: 3)

NUTRITIONAL INFO PER SERVING:

Calories: 312, Protein: 34.9g, Carbs: 3.7g, Fats: 17g

INGREDIENTS:

1 lb shrimp, peeled, deveined

3 tbsp olive oil

½ cup lemon juice

1 garlic clove, crushed

1 tsp fresh rosemary, crushed

1 tsp sea salt

DIRECTIONS:

1. Combine olive oil with lemon juice, crushed garlic, rosemary, and salt.
2. Using a kitchen brush, spread the mixture over the shrimp and place in a large Ziploc bag.
3. Cook en sous vide for 30 minutes at 135 degrees F.
4. Remove shrimp from bag and stir-fry them in a medium-hot skillet, about 5 minutes.
5. Enjoy!

Clams in Fresh Lime Juice

(Prep + Cook Time: 32 minutes | Serves: 2)

NUTRITIONAL INFO PER SERVING:

Calories: 318, Protein: 28.7g, Carbs: 6.8g, Fats: 41.7g

INGREDIENTS:

1 pound fresh Clams, debearded
1 medium-sized onion, chopped
Garlic cloves, crushed
½ cup lime juice
¼ cup fresh parsley, chopped
1 tbsp rosemary, finely chopped
2 tbsp olive oil

DIRECTIONS:

1. Place clams along with lime juice, garlic, onion, parsley, rosemary, and olive oil in a large Ziploc bag.
2. Cook en sous vide for 30 minutes at 122 degrees F.
3. Serve with mesclun salad.

Squid Rings

(Prep + Cook Time: 2 hours 5 minutes | Serves: 3)

NUTRITIONAL INFO PER SERVING:

Calories: 415, Protein: 20.9g, Carbs: 5g, Fats: 25.6g

INGREDIENTS:

2 cups squid rings

1 tbsp fresh rosemary

1 tsp salt

½ tsp ground black pepper

½ cup olive oil

DIRECTIONS:

1. Combine squid rings with rosemary, salt, pepper, and olive oil in a large clean plastic bag.
2. Seal the bag and shake a couple of times to coat well.
3. Transfer to a large Ziploc and seal the bag.
4. Cook en sous vide for 2 hours at 131 degrees F.
5. Remove from the water bath and serve.

Poultry

Aromatic Chicken

(Prep + Cook Time: 5 hours 35 minutes | Serves: 6)

NUTRITIONAL INFO PER SERVING:

Calories: 582, Protein: 82.7g, Carbs: 2.8g, Fats: 25.1g

INGREDIENTS:

1 five-pound chicken, whole

3 tbsp lemon juice

½ cup olive oil

6 bay leaves, dried

2 tbsp rosemary, crushed

3 tbsp thyme, dried

2 tbsp coconut oil

¼ cup lemon zest

3 garlic cloves, minced

DIRECTIONS:

1. Rinse well the chicken under cold running water and pat dry with a kitchen towel. Set aside.
2. In a small bowl, combine olive oil with salt, lemon juice, dried bay leaves, rosemary, and thyme.
3. Stuff the chicken's cavity with lemon slices and this mixture.
4. In another bowl, combine coconut oil with lemon zest and garlic. Loosen the skin of the chicken from the flesh.
5. Rub this mixture under the skin and place in a large plastic bag. Refrigerate for 30 minutes.
6. Remove from the refrigerator and place in a large Ziploc bag.
7. Cook en sous vide for 5 hours at 149 degrees F.

Mediterranean Chicken Thighs

(Prep + Cook Time: 1 hour 40 minutes | Serves: 3)

NUTRITIONAL INFO PER SERVING:

Calories: 334, Protein: 42.4g, Carbs: 3g, Fats: 16.1g

INGREDIENTS:

1 pound chicken thighs	3 garlic cloves, crushed
1 cup olive oil	1 tbsp cayenne pepper
½ cup lime juice	1 tsp dried oregano
½ cup parsley, finely chopped	1 tsp sea salt

DIRECTIONS:

1. Rinse the meat under cold running water and drain in a large colander. In a medium-sized bowl, combine olive oil with lime juice, chopped parsley, crushed garlic, cayenne pepper, oregano, and salt.
2. Submerge fillets in this mixture and cover. Refrigerate for 30 minutes. Remove the meat from the refrigerator and drain.
3. Place in a large Ziploc and cook en sous vide for 1 hour at 167 degrees F.

Turkey Breast with Pecans

(Prep + Cook Time: 2 hours 15 minutes | Serves: 6)

NUTRITIONAL INFO PER SERVING:

Calories: 356, Protein: 30.2g, Carbs: 10.1g, Fats: 22.2g

INGREDIENTS:

2 pounds turkey breast, sliced	2 garlic cloves, crushed
1 tbsp lemon zest	2 tbsp fresh parsley, chopped
1 cup pecans, finely chopped	3 cups chicken broth
1 tbsp thyme, finely chopped	3 tbsp olive oil

DIRECTIONS:

1. Rinse the meat under cold running water and drain in a colander. Rub with lemon zest and transfer to a large Ziploc bag along with chicken broth. Cook en sous vide for 2 hours at 149 degrees F. Remove from the water bath and set aside.
2. Heat the olive oil in a medium-sized skillet and add garlic, pecan nuts, parsley, and thyme. Give it a good stir and cook for 4-5 minutes.
3. Finally, add turkey to the frying pan and briefly brown on both sides, about 5 minutes. Serve immediate.

Chicken Thighs with Herbs

(Prep + Cook Time: 4 hours 10 minutes | Serves: 4)

NUTRITIONAL INFO PER SERVING:

Calories: 356, Protein: 44.6g, Carbs: 4.2g, Fats: 16.6g

INGREDIENTS:

1 pound chicken thighs
1 cup extra virgin olive oil
¼ cup apple cider vinegar
3 garlic cloves, crushed
½ cup lemon juice

1 tbsp fresh basil, chopped
2 tbsp fresh thyme, chopped
1 tbsp fresh rosemary, chopped
1 tsp cayenne pepper
1 tsp salt

DIRECTIONS:

1. Rinse the meat under cold running water and place in a large colander to drain. Set aside.
2. In a large bowl, combine olive oil with apple cider vinegar, garlic, lemon juice, basil, thyme, rosemary, salt, and cayenne pepper.
3. Submerge thighs into this mixture and refrigerate for 1 hour. Remove the meat from the marinade and drain.
4. Place in a Ziploc bag and cook for 3 hours at 149 degrees F.

Garlic Chicken with Mushrooms

(Prep + Cook Time: 2 hours 10 minutes | Serves: 6)

NUTRITIONAL INFO PER SERVING:

Calories: 505, Protein: 53.2g, Carbs: 30.5g, Fats: 21.1g

INGREDIENTS:

2 lb chicken thighs, skinless	½ tsp onion powder
1 lb cremini mushrooms, sliced	½ tsp sage leaves, dried
1 cup chicken stock	¼ tsp cayenne pepper
1 garlic clove, crushed	¼ tsp black pepper
4 tbsp olive oil	¼ tsp salt

DIRECTIONS:

1. Wash the thighs thoroughly under cold running water.
2. Pat dry with a kitchen paper and set aside.
3. In a large skillet, heat the olive oil over medium-high heat.
4. Brown both sides of the chicken thighs for 2 minutes per side.
5. Remove from the skillet and set aside.
6. Now, add garlic and sauté until lightly brown, about 2 minutes.
7. Stir in the mushrooms, pour in the stock and cook until it reaches to a boil. Remove from the pan and set aside.
8. Season the thighs with salt, pepper, cayenne pepper, and onion powder.
9. Place in a large Ziploc bag along with mushrooms and sage.
10. Seal the bag, and cook en sous vide for 2 hours at 149 degrees F.

Pepper Chicken Salad

(Prep + Cook Time: 70 minutes | Serves: 4)

NUTRITIONAL INFO PER SERVING:

Calories: 180, Protein: 8.3g, Carbs: 10.5g, Fats: 12.3g

INGREDIENTS:

1 lb chicken breast, boneless and skinless

¼ cup vegetable oil

3 tbsp olive oil

1 medium-sized onion, chopped

6 cherry tomatoes, halved

½ tsp ground black pepper

1 tsp pink Himalayan salt

1 cup lettuce, finely chopped

2 tbsp lemon juice

½ tsp salt

DIRECTIONS:

1. Thoroughly rinse the meat under the cold water and pat dry using a kitchen paper.
2. With a sharp paring knife, cut the meat into bite-sized pieces and season with salt and black pepper. Place in a Ziploc bag along with vegetable oil.
3. Cook for 1 hour at 149 degrees F.
4. Remove from the bag and chill to room temperature.
5. Mix the lettuce, cherry tomatoes, and onion in a large bowl.
6. Add chicken breast and season with olive oil, lemon juice, and salt to taste.
7. Serve cold.

Lemon Chicken with Mint

(Prep + Cook Time: 2 hours 40 minutes | Serves: 3)

NUTRITIONAL INFO PER SERVING:

Calories: 340, Protein: 44.2g, Carbs: 2.2g, Fats: 16.1g

INGREDIENTS:

1 lb thighs, boneless, skinless	1 tsp ginger
¼ cup oil	1 tbsp cayenne pepper
1 tbsp lemon juice	1 tsp fresh mint, chopped
2 garlic cloves, crushed	½ tsp salt

DIRECTIONS:

1. In a small bowl, combine olive oil with lemon juice, garlic, ground ginger, mint, cayenne pepper, and salt.
2. Generously brush each chicken thigh with this mixture and refrigerate for 30 minutes.
3. Remove thighs from the refrigerator and pat dry with a kitchen paper. Place in a large Ziploc bag and cook for 2 hours at 149 degrees F.
4. Remove from the Ziploc and serve immediately with spring onions. Enjoy!

Turkey Breast with Cloves

(Prep + Cook Time: 1 hour 35 minutes | Serves: 6)

NUTRITIONAL INFO PER SERVING:

Calories: 453, Protein: 26.2g, Carbs: 7.5g, Fats: 36.5g

INGREDIENTS:

2 pounds turkey breast, sliced	2 tbsp lemon juice
2 garlic cloves, minced	1 tsp fresh rosemary, chopped
1 cup olive oil	1 tsp cloves, minced
2 tbsp Dijon mustard	Salt and pepper to taste

DIRECTIONS:

1. In a large bowl, combine olive oil, with mustard, lemon juice, garlic, rosemary, cloves, salt, and pepper.
2. Mix until well incorporated and add turkey slices.
3. Soak well and refrigerate for 30 minutes before cooking.
4. Remove from the fridge and transfer to two Ziploc bags.
5. Seal the bags and cook en sous vide for 1 hour at 149 degrees F for tender and juicy, or 167 degrees F for well done.
6. Remove from the water bath and serve.

Artichoke Stuffed Chicken

(Prep + Cook Time: 3 hours 10 minutes | Serves: 6)

NUTRITIONAL INFO PER SERVING:

Calories: 505, Protein: 53.2g, Carbs: 30.5g, Fats: 21.1g

INGREDIENTS:

2 lb chicken breasts
½ cup chopped baby spinach
8 garlic cloves, crushed
10 artichoke hearts
1 tsp salt
½ tsp white pepper
1 cup fresh parsley, chopped
4 tbsp olive oil

DIRECTIONS:

1. Combine artichoke, pepper, fresh parsley, and garlic in a food processor. Blend until completely smooth. Pulse again and gradually add oil until well incorporated.
2. Stuff each breast with equal amounts of artichoke mixture and chopped baby spinach.
3. Slowly fold the breast fillet back together and secure the edge with a wooden skewer. Season with salt and white pepper and transfer to separate Ziploc bags.
4. Seal the bags and cook en sous vide for 3 hours at 149 degrees F.

Chicken Pudding with Artichoke Hearts

(Prep + Cook Time: 1 hour 20 minutes | Serves: 3)

NUTRITIONAL INFO PER SERVING:

Calories: 467, Protein: 46g, Carbs: 7.1g, Fats: 28.3g

INGREDIENTS:

1 lb chicken breast, skinless

2 medium-sized artichokes

2 tbsp butter

2 tbsp extra virgin olive oil

1 lemon

A handful parsley, chopped

1 tsp salt

¼ tsp ground black pepper

½ tsp chili pepper

DIRECTIONS:

1. Thoroughly rinse the meat and pat dry with a kitchen paper. Cut the chicken into smaller pieces and remove the bones. Rub with olive oil and set aside.
2. Heat a pan over medium heat. Add the meat.
3. Cook for about 3 minutes to get it a little golden on both sides. Remove from the heat and transfer to a large Ziploc bag. Seal the bag, and cook en sous vide for 1 hour at 149 degrees F.
4. Meanwhile, prepare the artichoke. Cut the lemon into halves and squeeze the juice in a small bowl.
5. Divide the juice in half and set aside.
6. Using a sharp paring knife, trim off the outer leaves until you reach the yellow and soft ones.
7. Trim off the green outer skin around the artichoke base and steam.
8. Cut artichoke into half-inch pieces. Rub with half of the lemon juice and place in a heavy-bottomed pot.
9. Add enough water to cover and cook until completely fork-tender, about 7-8 minutes.

10. Remove from the heat. Chill for a while – to room temperature. Cut each piece into thin strips.
11. Now combine artichokes with chicken meat in a large bowl. Stir in salt, pepper, and the remaining lemon juice.
12. Melt the butter over medium heat and drizzle over pudding. Sprinkle with some chili pepper and serve.

Chicken with Sun-Dried Tomatoes

(Prep + Cook Time: 1 hour 5 minutes | Serves: 3)

NUTRITIONAL INFO PER SERVING:
Calories: 346, Protein: 44.3g, Carbs: 4.1g, Fats: 16g

INGREDIENTS:

1 lb chicken breasts, skinless and boneless

½ cup sun-dried tomatoes

1 tsp raw honey

2 tbsp fresh lemon juice

1 tbsp fresh mint, finely chopped

1 tbsp minced shallots

1 tbsp olive oil

½ tsp salt

¼ tsp ground black pepper

DIRECTIONS:

1. Rinse the chicken breasts under cold running water and pat dry with a kitchen paper. Set aside.
2. In a bowl, combine lemon juice, honey, mint, shallots, olive oil, salt, and pepper. Mix together until well incorporated.
3. Add chicken breasts and sun-dried tomatoes.
4. Shake to coat all well. Transfer all to a large Ziploc bag.
5. Press the bag to remove the air and seal the lid.
6. Cook en sous vide for 1 hour at 167 degrees F.
7. Remove from the water bath and serve immediately.

Sweet Orange Chicken Thighs

(Prep + Cook Time: 3 hours | Serves: 4)

NUTRITIONAL INFO PER SERVING:

Calories: 451, Protein: 67.8g, Carbs: 8.7g, Fats: 14.3g

INGREDIENTS:

2 lb chicken thighs, whole
2 small chili peppers, chopped
1 cup chicken broths
½ cup orange juice
1 tsp orange extract, liquid
2 tbsp olive oil
1 tsp barbecue seasoning mix
1 onion, chopped

DIRECTIONS:

1. Heat the olive oil in a large saucepan.
2. Add onion and stir-fry for 3 minutes, over a medium temperature until translucent.
3. In a food processor, combine the orange juice with chili pepper, and orange extract.
4. Pulse until well combined. Pour the mixture into a saucepan and reduce the heat. Simmer for 10 more minutes.
5. Rinse well chicken under cold running water.
6. Coat with barbecue seasoning mix and place in a saucepan.
7. Add chicken broth and continue to cook until half of the liquid evaporates.
8. Remove from the heat and coat each chicken thigh with sauce. Place in a large Ziploc bag and seal.
9. Cook en sous vide for 2 hours and 45 minutes at 150 degrees F.

Chicken Stew with Mushrooms

(Prep + Cook Time: 2 hours 15 minutes | Serves: 2)

NUTRITIONAL INFO PER SERVING:

Calories: 242, Protein: 31.3g, Carbs: 11.2g, Fats: 7.8g

INGREDIENTS:

2 chicken thighs
½ cup fire-roasted tomatoes
½ cup chicken stock
1 tbsp tomato paste
½ cup button mushrooms
1 medium-sized celery stalk
1 small carrot

1 small onion
1 tbsp dried basil, finely chopped
1 garlic clove, crushed
½ tsp salt
¼ tsp black pepper
1 tbsp olive oil

DIRECTIONS:

1. Rinse the thighs and remove the skin.
2. Rub with salt and pepper. Set aside. Clean the vegetables.
3. Peel and chop the onion, slice the carrot, and chop the mushrooms.
4. Chop the celery stalk into half-inch long pieces.
5. Place the meat in a large Ziploc bag along with onion, carrot, mushrooms, celery stalk, and fire roasted tomatoes.
6. Cook en sous vide for 2 hours at 150 degrees F.
7. Remove from the water bath and open the bag. The meat should be falling off the bone easily, so remove the bones.
8. Heat olive oil in a medium-sized saucepan, and add garlic.
9. Briefly fry for about 2 minutes, stirring constantly.
10. Now add chicken along with cooked vegetables, and chicken stock. Cook for 5 minutes and serve.

Chicken Wings with Ginger

(Prep + Cook Time: 2 hours 20 minutes | Serves: 4)

NUTRITIONAL INFO PER SERVING:

Kcal: 562, Protein: 66.1g, Carbs: 4g, Fats: 29.8g

INGREDIENTS:

2 pounds chicken wings

¼ cup extra virgin olive oil

4 garlic cloves

1 tbsp rosemary, chopped

1 tsp white pepper

1 tsp cayenne pepper

1 tbsp fresh thyme, chopped

1 tbsp fresh ginger, grated

¼ cup lime juice

½ cup apple cider vinegar

DIRECTIONS:

1. Rinse the chicken wings under cold running water and drain in a large colander.
2. In a large bowl, combine olive oil with garlic, rosemary, white pepper, cayenne pepper, thyme, ginger, lime juice, and apple cider vinegar.
3. Submerge wings in this mixture. Refrigerate for 1 hour.
4. Transfer the wings along with the marinade to a large Ziploc bag.
5. Seal the bag and cook en sous vide for 1 hour and 15 minutes at 149 degrees F.
6. Remove from the Ziploc bag and brown in a saucepan over medium heat for 5 minutes.
7. Serve and enjoy!

Stuffed Chicken Breasts

(Prep + Cook Time: 1 hour 35 minutes | Serves: 5)

NUTRITIONAL INFO PER SERVING:

Calories: 397, Protein: 52.8g, Carbs: 0.9g, Fats: 19.1g

INGREDIENTS:

2 lb chicken breasts, skinless and boneless

2 tbsp fresh parsley, chopped

2 tbsp fresh basil, chopped

1 large egg

½ cup spring onions, chopped

½ tsp salt

¼ tsp black pepper, ground

2 tbsp olive oil

DIRECTIONS:

1. Wash the chicken breasts thoroughly and pat dry with a kitchen paper.
2. Rub some salt and pepper and set aside.
3. In a medium-sized bowl, combine egg, basil, and spring onions.
4. Stir until well incorporated.
5. Place the chicken breasts on a clean surface and spoon the egg mixture onto the middle.
6. Fold the breasts over to seal.
7. Gently place each breast in a separate Ziploc bag and press to remove the air.
8. Seal the bags and place in a water bath.
9. Cook en sous vide for 1 hour and 30 minutes at 145 degrees F.
10. Gently remove the chicken breasts from the bags.
11. Heat the oil in a large skillet over medium-high heat.
12. Add chicken breasts and brown for about 1-2 minutes on each side.
13. Serve sprinkled with parsley.

Cherry Chicken Bites

(Prep + Cook Time: 1 hour 35 minutes | Serves: 3)

NUTRITIONAL INFO PER SERVING:

Calories: 210, Protein: 9.9g, Carbs: 7.7g, Fats: 16.6g

INGREDIENTS:

1 lb chicken breast, boneless, skinless

1 cup red bell pepper

1 cup green bell pepper

1 cup cherry tomatoes, whole

1 cup olive oil

1 tsp Italian seasoning mix

1 tsp cayenne pepper

½ tsp dried oregano

1 tsp salt

½ tsp ground black pepper

DIRECTIONS:

1. Rinse the meat under cold running water and pat dry with a kitchen paper.
2. Cut into bite-sized pieces and set aside.
3. Wash the bell peppers and cut them into chunks.
4. Wash the cherry tomatoes and remove the green stems. Set aside.
5. In a medium-sized bowl, combine olive oil with Italian seasoning, cayenne, salt, and pepper.
6. Stir until well incorporated.
7. Now, add the meat and coat well with the marinade.
8. Set aside for 30 minutes to allow flavors to meld and penetrate the meat.
9. Place the meat along with vegetables in a large Ziploc bag.
10. Add 3 tablespoons of the marinade and seal the bag.
11. Cook en sous vide for 1 hour at 149 degrees F.

White Wine Veal, Chicken and Mushroom Chops

(Prep + Cook Time: 3 hours 10 minutes | Serves: 4)

NUTRITIONAL INFO PER SERVING:

Calories: 388, Protein: 37.6g, Carbs: 12.5g, Fats: 20g

INGREDIENTS:

1 pound lean veal cuts

1 lb chicken breast, boneless, skinless

4 cups button mushrooms

3 large carrots, sliced

1 cup celery root, chopped

2 tbsp butter, softened

1 tbsp extra-virgin olive oil

1 tbsp cayenne pepper

1 tsp salt

½ tsp ground black pepper

¼ cup white wine

A handful celery leaves, chopped

DIRECTIONS:

1. Thoroughly wash the veal and chicken under the running water. Cut into bite-sized pieces and set aside.
2. Wash and slice the mushrooms.
3. In a large bowl, combine veal and chicken with mushrooms, carrots, celery root, olive oil, cayenne pepper, salt, and black pepper. Stir well and transfer to a large Ziploc.
4. Seal the bag and cook en sous vide for 3 hours at 144 degrees F for medium rare, or at 158 degrees F for well done.
5. Melt the butter in a large saucepan. Add the meat mixture to the pan and stir-fry for 1 minute.
6. Pour in ¼ cup of wine and bring it to a boil. Cook for 1 more minute and remove from the heat.
7. Sprinkle with chopped celery leaves and serve warm.

Turkey Salad with Cucumber

(Prep + Cook Time: 2 hours 10 minutes | Serves: 3)

NUTRITIONAL INFO PER SERVING:

Calories: 415, Protein: 46.1g, Carbs: 9.2g, Fats: 21.3g

INGREDIENTS:

1 lb turkey breasts, boneless
½ cup chicken broth
2 garlic cloves, minced
2 tbsp olive oil
1 tsp salt
¼ tsp Cayenne pepper

2 bay leaves
1 medium tomato, chopped
1 large red bell pepper, chopped
1 medium-sized cucumber
½ tsp Italian seasoning

DIRECTIONS:

1. Using a sharp paring knife, gently remove the skin from the breast. Cut the meat into half-inch thick slices and then into bite-sized pieces.
2. Rinse thoroughly and season with salt, and cayenne pepper.
3. Place in a large Ziploc along with chicken broth, garlic, and bay leaves.
4. Seal the bag and cook en sous vide for 2 hours at 157 degrees F.
5. Remove from the water bath, remove and discard the bay leaves, and set aside.
6. Mix bell pepper, tomato, and cucumber in a large bowl.
7. Add turkey breast and season with Italian seasoning mix and olive oil.
8. Toss well to combine and serve immediately.

Chicken Thighs with Carrot Puree

(Prep + Cook Time: 2 hours 15 minutes | Serves: 5

NUTRITIONAL INFO PER SERVING:

Calories: 420, Protein: 54.7g, Carbs: 3.2g, Fats: 19.6g

INGREDIENTS:

2 pounds chicken thighs

1 cup carrots, thinly sliced

2 tbsp olive oil

¼ cup finely chopped onion

2 cups of chicken broth

2 tbsp fresh parsley, chopped

2 crushed garlic cloves

1 tsp salt

¼ tsp ground black pepper

DIRECTIONS:

1. Wash the chicken thighs under cold running water and pat dry with a kitchen paper. Set aside.
2. In a large bowl, combine olive oil, parsley, salt, and pepper.
3. Stir well and generously brush the thighs with this mixture.
4. Place in a large Ziploc bag and add chicken broth. Press the bag to remove the air.
5. Seal and place in a water bath.
6. Cook en sous vide for 2 hours minutes at 150 degrees F.
7. Meanwhile, prepare the carrots. Transfer to a blender and process until pureed. Set aside.
8. When done, remove the thighs from the water bath. Remove from the bag but reserve the broth liquid.
9. Heat a large skillet over medium-high heat.
10. Add garlic and stir-fry for about 1-2 minutes.
11. Add chicken thighs and cook for 2-3 minutes, turning occasionally. Sprinkle with parsley, salt, and pepper.
12. Cook for 2 minutes more and then add broth.
13. Bring it to a boil and remove from the heat.
14. Transfer the thighs to a serving plate and serve with carrot puree.

Chicken Breast with Vegetables

Prep Time: 2 hours 10 minutes | Serves: 2)

NUTRITIONAL INFO PER SERVING:

Calories: 173, Protein: 16.4g, Carbs: 18g, Fats: 4.4g

INGREDIENTS:

1 lb chicken breast, boneless and skinless

1 cup red bell pepper, sliced

1 cup bell pepper, sliced

1 cup zucchini, sliced

½ cup onion, finely chopped

1 cup cauliflower florets

½ cup lemon juice

½ cup chicken stock

½ tsp ground ginger

1 tsp pink Himalayan salt

DIRECTIONS:

1. In a bowl, combine lemon juice with chicken stock, ginger, and salt. Stir well and add sliced vegetables. Set aside.
2. Rinse the chicken breast under cold running water.
3. Cut the meat into bite-sized pieces. Combine with other ingredients and stir well.
4. Transfer to a large Ziploc bag and seal it. Cook for 2 hours at 157 degrees F. Serve immediately.

Italian Chicken Fingers

(Prep + Cook Time: 2 hours 10 minutes | Serves: 3)

NUTRITIONAL INFO PER SERVING:

Calories: 424, Protein: 17.5g, Carbs: 17.5g, Fats: 33.3g

INGREDIENTS:

1 lb chicken breast, boneless skinless

1 cup almond flour

1 tsp minced garlic

Salt and pepper to taste

½ tsp cayenne pepper

2 tbsp mixed Italian herbs

2 eggs, beaten

¼ cup olive oil

DIRECTIONS:

1. Rinse the meat under cold running water and pat dry with a kitchen paper.
2. Season with mixed Italian herbs and place in a large Ziploc.
3. Seal the bag and cook en sous vide for 2 hours at 157 degrees F. Remove from the water bath and set aside.
4. Now combine together flour, salt, cayenne, Italian herbs, and pepper in a bowl and set aside.
5. In a separate bowl, beat the eggs and set aside.
6. Heat olive oil in a large skillet, over medium-high heat.
7. Dip the chicken into the beaten egg and coat with the flour mixture. Fry for 5 minutes on each side, or until golden brown.

Mustard Drumsticks

(Prep + Cook Time: 2 hours 50 minutes | Serves: 5

NUTRITIONAL INFO PER SERVING:

Calories: 658, Protein: 53.5g, Carbs: 0.8g, Fats: 53.5g

INGREDIENTS:

2 pounds chicken drumsticks
¼ cup Dijon mustard
2 garlic cloves, crushed

2 tbsp coconut aminos
1 tsp pink Himalayan salt
½ tsp ground black pepper

DIRECTIONS:

1. Rinse drumsticks under cold running water.
2. Drain in a large colander and set aside.
3. In a small bowl, combine Dijon mustard with crushed garlic, coconut aminos, salt, and pepper.
4. Spread the mixture over the meat with a kitchen brush and place in a large Ziploc bag.
5. Seal the bag and cook en sous vide for 2 hours and 45 minutes at 157 degrees F.

Turkey in Orange Sauce

(Prep + Cook Time: 3 hours 25 minutes | Serves: 2)

NUTRITIONAL INFO PER SERVING:

Calories: 303, Protein: 39.2g, Carbs: 12.8g, Fats: 9.9g

INGREDIENTS:

1 lb turkey breasts, skinless boneless

1 tbsp butter

3 tbsp fresh orange juice

½ cup chicken stock

1 tsp ground Cayenne pepper

½ tsp salt

¼ tsp black pepper, ground

DIRECTIONS:

1. Rinse the turkey breasts under cold running water and pat dry. Set aside.
2. In a medium bowl, combine orange juice, chicken stock, Cayenne pepper, salt, and pepper.
3. Mix well and place the meat into this marinade. Refrigerate for 20 minutes.
4. Now, place the meat along with the marinade into a large Ziploc bag and cook en sous vide for 3 hours minutes at 140 degrees F.
5. In a medium nonstick saucepan, melt the butter over medium-high temperature.
6. Remove the meat from the bag and add it to the saucepan.
7. Fry for about 2 minutes and remove from the heat.

Vegetables

Brussel Sprouts in White Wine

(Prep + Cook Time: 40 minutes | Serves: 4)

NUTRITIONAL INFO PER SERVING:
Calories: 279, Protein: 3.2g, Carbs: 8.3g, Fats: 25.6g

INGREDIENTS:

1 lb Brussels sprouts

½ cup extra virgin olive oil

½ cup white wine

1 tsp salt

2 tbsp fresh parsley, chopped

¼ tsp ground black pepper

2 garlic cloves, crushed

DIRECTIONS:

1. Rinse Brussels sprouts under cold running water. Drain in a large colander and transfer to a clean working surface.
2. Using a sharp paring knife, trim the outer leaves and place in a large Ziploc bag with three tablespoons of olive oil.
3. Cook en sous vide for 30 minutes at 180 degrees F. Remove from the bag.
4. In a large, non-stick grill pan, heat the remaining olive oil.
5. Add Brussels sprouts, crushed garlic, salt, and pepper.
6. Briefly grill, shaking the pan a couple of times until lightly charred on all sides.
7. Add wine and bring it to a boil. Stir well and remove from the heat.
8. Top with finely chopped parsley and serve.
9. Enjoy!

Braised Greens with Mint

(Prep + Cook Time: 20 minutes | Serves: 2)

NUTRITIONAL INFO PER SERVING:

Calories: 191, Protein: 5.8g, Carbs: 12.8g, Fats: 15.1g

INGREDIENTS:

½ cup fresh chicory, torn

½ cup asparagus, chopped

½ cup Swiss chard, torn

¼ cup fresh mint, chopped

¼ cup arugula, torn

2 garlic cloves, minced

½ tsp salt

4 tbsp lemon juice

2 tbsp olive oil

DIRECTIONS:

1. Fill a large pot with salted water and add greens. Bring it to a boil and cook for 3 minutes.
2. Remove from the heat and drain in a large colander.
3. Gently squeeze with your hands and using a sharp knife chop the greens.
4. Transfer to a large Ziploc and cook en sous vide for 10 minutes at 162 degrees F.
5. Remove from the water bath and set aside.
6. Heat the olive oil over medium-high heat in a large skillet. Add garlic and stir-fry for 1 minute.
7. Add greens and season with salt. Give it a good stir and remove from the heat.
8. Sprinkle with fresh lemon juice and serve warm or even cold.

Beet Spinach Salad

(Prep + Cook Time: 2 hours 45 minutes | Serves: 3)

NUTRITIONAL INFO PER SERVING:

Calories: 163, Protein: 2.1g, Carbs: 19.7g, Fats: 13.4g

INGREDIENTS:

2 beets

1 cup fresh spinach

2 tbsp olive oil

1 tbsp lemon juice

1 tsp balsamic vinegar

2 garlic cloves, crushed

1 tbsp butter

½ tsp salt

¼ tsp black pepper, ground

DIRECTIONS:

1. Rinse well and clean beets. Chop into bite-sized pieces and place in a Ziploc along with butter and crushed garlic.
2. Cook en sous vide for 2 hours at 185 degrees F. Remove from the water bath and set aside to cool.
3. Rinse and clean spinach. Drain well in a colander and chop with a sharp knife.
4. Boil a large pot of water and place spinach in it. Cook for one minute, and then remove from the heat. Drain well.
5. Transfer to a Ziploc and cook en sous vide for 10 minutes at 180 degrees F.
6. Remove from the water bath and cool completely.
7. Place in a large bowl and add cooked beets.
8. Season with salt, pepper, balsamic vinegar, olive oil, and lemon juice.

Leek with Garlic and Eggs

(Prep + Cook Time: 25 minutes | Serves: 2)

NUTRITIONAL INFO PER SERVING:

Calories: 379, Protein: 14.5g, Carbs: 15.8g, Fats: 30g

INGREDIENTS:

2 cups fresh leek, chopped

5 garlic cloves, whole

1 tbsp butter

2 tbsp extra virgin olive oil

4 large eggs

1 tsp salt

DIRECTIONS:

1. Whisk together eggs, butter, and salt.
2. Transfer to a Ziploc bag and cook en sous vide for 10 minutes at 165 degrees F.
3. Gently transfer to a plate.
4. Heat the oil in a large skillet over medium-high heat.
5. Add garlic and chopped leek. Stir-fry for 10 minutes.
6. Remove from the heat.
7. Serve the eggs topped with leeks.

Spinach and Mushroom Quiche

(Prep + Cook Time: 50 minutes | Serves: 2)

NUTRITIONAL INFO PER SERVING:

Calories: 283, Protein: 21.4g, Carbs: 6.3g, Fats: 19.9g

INGREDIENTS:

1 cup Cremini mushrooms,

1 cup Fresh spinach

2 large eggs, beaten

2 tbsp whole milk

1 garlic clove, minced

¼ cup Parmesan cheese, grated

1 tbsp butter

½ tsp salt

DIRECTIONS:

1. Wash the mushrooms under cold running water and thinly slice them. Set aside.
2. Wash the spinach thoroughly and roughly chop it.
3. In a large Ziploc bag, place mushrooms, spinach, milk, garlic, and salt.
4. Seal the bag and cook en sous vide for 40 minutes at 140 degrees F.
5. Melt the butter in a large saucepan over medium-high heat.
6. Remove the vegetable mixture from the bag and add it to a saucepan. Cook for 1 minute, and then add beaten eggs.
7. Stir well until incorporated and cook until eggs are set.
8. Just before removing from the heat, sprinkle with grated cheese. Serve warm.

Braised Swiss Chard with Lime

(Prep + Cook Time: 15 minutes | Serves: 4)

NUTRITIONAL INFO PER SERVING:

Calories: 166, Protein: 4.2g, Carbs: 9g, Fats: 14.6g

INGREDIENTS:

2 pounds Swiss chard
4 tbsp extra virgin olive oil
2 garlic cloves, crushed

1 whole lime, juiced
2 tsp sea salt

DIRECTIONS:

1. Thoroughly rinse Swiss chard and drain in a colander.
2. Using a sharp paring knife roughly chop and transfer to a large bowl.
3. Stir in olive oil, crushed garlic, lime juice, and sea salt. Transfer to a large Ziploc bag and seal.
4. Cook en sous vide for 10 minutes at 180 degrees F.

Tomato Stuffed Mushrooms

(Prep + Cook Time: 55 minutes | Serves: 4)

NUTRITIONAL INFO PER SERVING:

Calories: 191, Protein: 23.9g, Carbs: 14.8g, Fats: 4g

INGREDIENTS:

2 pounds Cremini mushrooms
1 yellow bell pepper, chopped
2 tomatoes, chopped
2 spring onions, finely chopped

1 ¾ cup lean ground beef
3 tbsp olive oil
1 tsp salt

DIRECTIONS:

1. Steam the mushrooms and place the caps aside.
2. Chop up the mushroom stems and set aside.
3. Heat olive oil in a large skillet.
4. Add onions and sauté for 2 minutes.
5. Add beef, mushrooms stems, tomatoes, salt, and cook for 5-6 more minutes, stirring constantly.
6. Place the mushroom caps on a clean work surface and drizzle with oil.
7. Scoop the beef mixture into each cap and place in a large Ziploc bag.
8. Cook en sous vide for 45 minutes at 141 degrees F.

Ginger and Spring Onion Eggs

(Prep + Cook Time: 27 minutes | Serves: 2)

NUTRITIONAL INFO PER SERVING:

Calories: 358, Protein: 25.7g, Carbs: 4.2g, Fats: 27g

INGREDIENTS:

8 free-range eggs, beaten
½ cup spring onions
1 tsp ginger, freshly grated

1 tbsp extra-virgin olive oil
¼ tsp pink Himalayan salt
¼ tsp black pepper, ground

DIRECTIONS:

1. In a medium bowl, whisk the eggs, ginger, salt, and pepper.
2. Transfer the mixture to a Ziploc bag and seal.
3. Cook en sous vide for 20 minutes at 165 degrees F.
4. Heat the oil in a small saucepan over medium-high temperature.
5. Add spring onions and cook for 2 minutes.
6. Remove from the heat.
7. When set, transfer the egg mixture to a serving plate and shape the omelet.
8. Top with onions and fold the omelet.
9. Serve immediately.

Desserts

Chocolate Pudding

(Prep + Cook Time: 45 minutes | Servings: 4)

NUTRITIONAL INFO PER SERVING:

Calories: 850, Protein: 19g, Carbs: 19g, Fats: 79g

INGREDIENTS:

½ cup Milk

1 cup Chocolate Chips

3 Egg Yolks

½ cup Heavy Cream

4 tbsp Cocoa Powder

3 tbsp Sugar

¼ tsp Salt

DIRECTIONS:

1. Whisk the yolks along with the sugar, milk, heavy cream, and salt. Stir in the cocoa powder and chocolate chips.
2. Divide the mixture between 4 jars.
3. Preheat your Sous Vide to 185 degrees F. Seal and immerse the jars in the water. Cook for 40 minutes. Let cool before serving.

Apple Pie

(Prep + Cook Time: 1 hour 20 minutes | Servings: 8)

NUTRITIONAL INFO PER SERVING:

Calories: 205, Protein: 2g, Carbs: 24g, Fats: 11g

INGREDIENTS:

1 pound Apples, cubed

6 ounces Puff Pastry

1 Egg Yolk, whisked

4 tbsp Sugar

2 tbsp Lemon Juice

1 tbsp Cornstarch

1 tsp ground Ginger

2 tbsp Butter, melted

¼ tsp Nutmeg

¼ tsp Cinnamon

DIRECTIONS:

1. Preheat your oven to 365 degrees F. Roll the pastry into a circle. Brush it with the butter and place in the oven. Cook for 15 minutes.
2. Combine all the remaining ingredients in a Ziploc bag. Seal and immerse in water at 180 degrees F.
3. Cook for 45 minutes. Top the cooked pie crust with the apple mixture. Return to the oven and cook for 15 more minutes.

Sugar-Free Chocolate Chip Cookies

(Prep + Cook Time: 3 hours 35 minutes | Servings: 6)

NUTRITIONAL INFO PER SERVING:

Calories: 276, Protein: 5g, Carbs: 18g, Fats: 20g

INGREDIENTS:

⅓ cup sugar-free Chocolate Chips

7 tbsp Heavy Cream

2 Eggs

½ cup Flour

½ tsp Baking Soda

4 tbsp Butter, melted

¼ tsp Salt

1 tbsp Lemon Juice

DIRECTIONS:

1. Beat the eggs along with the cream, lemon juice, salt, and baking soda. Stir in the flour and butter. Fold in the chocolate chips.
2. Preheat the Sous Vide to 194 degrees F. Divide the dough between 6 ramekins. Wrap them well with plastic foil.
3. Place the ramekins in the water bath. Cook for 3 ½ hours.
4. Remove the ramekins from the bath. Let cool slightly before serving.

Vanilla Ice Cream

(Prep + Cook Time: 5 hours | Servings: 4)

NUTRITIONAL INFO PER SERVING:

Calories: 290, Protein: 7g, Carbs: 18g, Fats: 20g

INGREDIENTS:

6 Egg Yolks

½ cup Brown Sugar

1 ½ tsp Vanilla Extract

2 cups Half and Half

DIRECTIONS:

1. Preheat the Sous Vide to 180 degrees F.
2. In your food processor, whisk all of the ingredients together until smooth and creamy, and place in a Ziploc bag.
3. Seal the bag and immerse in the preheated Sous Vide.
4. Cook for 1 hour. Make sure there are no clumps before transferring the mixture to a container with a lid.
5. Remove and unseal the bag. Let cool in ice bath. Pour the mixture into an ice cream machine, and process according to the maker's instructions.
6. Place in the freezer for 4 hours until firm. Scoop into bowls and serve.

Rice Pudding with Rum Cranberries

(Prep + Cook Time: 4 hours 10 minutes | Servings: 6)

NUTRITIONAL INFO PER SERVING:

Calories: 465, Protein: 9g, Carbs: 87g, Fats: 4g

INGREDIENTS:

2 cups Rice

3 cups Milk

½ cup dried Cranberries soaked in ½ cup of Rum overnight and

drained

1 tsp Cinnamon

½ cup Brown Sugar

DIRECTIONS:

1. Preheat the Sous Vide to 170 degrees F.
2. Combine all of the ingredients in a bowl. Divide the mixture among 6 small jars.
3. Seal them and immerse in the water. Cook for 4 hours.
4. Once the timer has stopped, remove the jars from the bath.
5. Serve warm or chilled.

Crème Brulee with Blueberries

(Prep + Cook Time: 2 hours 35 minutes | Servings: 4)

NUTRITIONAL INFO PER SERVING:

Calories: 493, Protein: 5g, Carbs: 10g, Fats: 48g

INGREDIENTS:

2 cups Heavy Cream
4 Egg Yolks
¼ cup Sugar

1 tsp Vanilla Extract
Zest from 1 Orange
1 cup of fresh blueberries

DIRECTIONS:

1. Set your Sous Vide to 180 degrees F.
2. Whisk together all the ingredients and pour the mixture into 4 shallow jars.
3. Seal the jars and submerge in the preheated water bath.
4. Cook for 30 minutes.
5. Once the timer has stopped, remove the jars and refrigerate for 2 hours.
6. Unseal the jars and sprinkle sugar on top of each custard.
7. Place under broiler until they become caramelized.
8. Serve garnished with fresh raspberries

Savory Bread Pudding

(Prep + Cook Time: 2 hours and 15 minutes | Servings: 8)

NUTRITIONAL INFO PER SERVING:

Calories: 265, Protein: 10g, Carbs: 21g, Fats: 15g

INGREDIENTS:

1 cup Milk

1 cup Heavy Cream

10 ounces White Bread

4 Eggs

2 tbsp Butter, melted

1 tbsp Flour

1 tbsp Corn Starch

4 tbsp Sugar

1 tsp Vanilla Extract

¼ tsp Salt

DIRECTIONS:

1. Preheat the water in the Sous Vide to 170 degrees F.
2. Chop the bread into small pieces and place in a Ziploc bag.
3. Beat the eggs along with the remaining ingredients in a large bowl until smooth. Pour the egg mixture over the bread and let soak for 15 minutes.
4. Distribute the mixture between 8 canning jars. Seal and submerge the jars in the water bath. Cook for 2 hours.
5. Remove the jars and refrigerate for 2 hours.

Lemony Muffins

(Prep + Cook Time: 3 hours and 45 minutes | Servings: 6)

NUTRITIONAL INFO PER SERVING:

Calories: 303, Protein: 6g, Carbs: 23g, Fats: 21g

INGREDIENTS:

2 Eggs

1 cup Flour

4 tbsp Sugar

1 tbsp Lemon Juice

1 tbsp Lemon Zest

⅓ cup Heavy Cream

2 Eggs

1 tsp Baking Soda

½ cup Butter

DIRECTIONS:

1. Beat the eggs and sugar until creamy. Gradually beat in the remaining ingredients. Divide the batter between 6 mason jars.
2. Preheat the water to 190 degrees F. Seal the jars and immerse them in the water. Cook for 3 ½ hours.
3. Let cool before serving.

Light Cottage Cheese Breakfast Pudding

(Prep + Cook Time: 3 hours 15 minutes | Servings: 3)

NUTRITIONAL INFO PER SERVING:

Calories: 426, Protein: 27g, Carbs: 22g, Fats: 24.6g

INGREDIENTS:

1 cup Cottage Cheese
5 Eggs
1 cup Milk
3 tbsp Sour Cream
4 tbsp Sugar

1 tsp Cardamom
1 tsp Orange Zest
1 tbsp Cornstarch
¼ tsp Salt

DIRECTIONS:

1. With an electric mixer, beat the eggs and sugar.
2. Beat in the zest, milk, and cornstarch.
3. Add the remaining ingredients and beat on medium for 5 minutes.
4. Grease 3 mason jars with cooking spray and divide the mixture between them. Seal.
5. Set the Sous Vide to 175 degrees F and place the jars inside.
6. Cook for 3 hours. Let cool before serving.

Citrus Curd

(Prep + Cook Time: 1 hour 35 minutes | Servings: 8)

NUTRITIONAL INFO PER SERVING:

Calories: 341, Protein: 4g, Carbs: 15g, Fats: 30g

INGREDIENTS:

1 cup Butter, melted

1 cup Sugar

12 Egg Yolks

2 Lemons

3 Oranges

¼ tsp Salt

DIRECTIONS:

1. Preheat the water to 180 degrees F.
1. Grate the zest from the lemons and oranges and place in a bowl. Squeeze the juice and add to the bowl as well.
2. Whisk the yolks, sugar, butter, and salt. Transfer to a Ziploc bag. Seal the bag and immerse in the preheated water. Cook for 1 hour.
3. Once the timer has stopped, remove and unseal the bag. Transfer the cooked citrus curd to a bowl, cover with a plastic wrap and place in an ice bath. Let chill thoroughly before serving.

Raspberry Mousse

(Prep + Cook Time: 1 hour 15 minutes | Servings: 6)

NUTRITIONAL INFO PER SERVING:

Calories: 216, Protein: 5g, Carbs: 22g, Fats: 13g

INGREDIENTS:

1 cup Raspberries

1 cup Milk

1 cup Cream Cheese

2 tbsp Cornstarch

½ cup Sugar

1 tbsp Flour

1 tsp ground Ginger

1 tbsp Cocoa Powder

DIRECTIONS:

1. Preheat the water to 170 degrees F.
1. Place all of the ingredients in a blender.
2. Blend until smooth and pale. Divide between 6 small jars.
3. Seal the jars and submerge in the water. Cook for 1 hour. Serve chilled.

Sous Vide Chocolate Cupcakes

(Prep + Cook Time: 3 hours 10 minutes | Servings: 6)

NUTRITIONAL INFO PER SERVING:

Calories: 211, Protein: 4g, Carbs: 23g, Fats: 11g

INGREDIENTS:

5 tbsp Butter, melted
1 Egg
3 tbsp Cocoa Powder
1 cup Flour
4 tbsp Sugar

½ cup Heavy Cream
1 tsp Baking Soda
1 tsp Vanilla Extract
1 tsp Apple Cider Vinegar
Pinch of Sea Salt

DIRECTIONS:

1. Whisk together the wet ingredients in one bowl.
2. Combine the dry ingredients in another bowl.
3. Combine the two mixtures gently.
4. Divide the batter between 6 small jars.
5. Preheat the water to 194 degrees F.
6. Seal the jars and place in the water. Cook for 3 hours.

Raisin-Stuffed Sweet Apples

(Prep + Cook Time: 2 hours 15 minutes | Servings: 4)

NUTRITIONAL INFO PER SERVING:
Calories: 325, Protein: 2.8g, Carbs: 38g, Fats: 19g

INGREDIENTS:

4 small Apples, cored	¼ tsp Nutmeg
1 ½ tbsp Raisins	½ tsp Cinnamon
4 tbsp Butter, softened	1 tbsp Sugar

DIRECTIONS:

1. Preheat the water to 170 degrees F. Combine the raisins, sugar, butter, cinnamon, and nutmeg.
2. Stuff the apples with the raisin mixture. Divide the apples between 2 Ziploc bags. Seal the bags and immerse them in the water. Cook for 2 hours.

Apple Cobbler

(Prep + Cook Time: 3 hours 40 minutes | Servings: 6)

NUTRITIONAL INFO PER SERVING:
Calories: 170, Protein: 2.4g, Carbs: 37g, Fats: 2g

INGREDIENTS:

1 cup Milk	7 tbsp Flour
2 Green Apples, cubed	4 tbsp Brown Sugar
1 tsp Butter	1 tsp ground Cardamom

DIRECTIONS:

1. Preheat the water to 190 degrees F. Whisk together the butter, sugar, milk, and cardamom. Stir in the flour gradually. Fold in the apples. Divide the mixture between 6 small jars. Seal the jars and place them in the water bath. Cook for 3 ½ hours.

Mini Strawberry Cheesecake Jars

(Prep + Cook Time: 90 minutes | Servings: 4)

NUTRITIONAL INFO PER SERVING:

Calories: 308, Protein: 15g, Carbs: 18g, Fats: 19g

INGREDIENTS:

4 Eggs

2 tbsp Milk

3 tbsp Strawberry Jam

½ cup Sugar

½ cup Cream Cheese

½ cup Cottage Cheese

1 tbsp Flour

1 tsp Lemon Zest

DIRECTIONS:

1. Preheat the water to 180 degrees F. Beat together the cheeses and sugar until fluffy. Beat in the eggs, one by one.
2. Add the remaining ingredients and beat until well combined. Divide between 4 jars. Seal and place in the water. Cook for 75 minutes. Chill and serve.

Wine and Cinnamon Poached Pears

(Prep + Cook Time: 90 minutes | Servings: 4)

NUTRITIONAL INFO PER SERVING:

Calories: 173, Protein: 1g, Carbs: 36g, Fats: 0.4g

INGREDIENTS:

4 Pears, peeled

2 Cinnamon Sticks

2 cups Red Wine

⅓ cup Sugar

3 Star Anise

DIRECTIONS:

1. Preheat the water to 175 degrees F. Combine the pears, wine, anise, sugar, and cinnamon in a Ziploc bag. Seal and immerse in the preheated water. Cook for 1 hour. Serve the pears drizzle with the wine sauce.

Mini Cheesecakes

(Prep + Cook Time: 1 hour 40 minutes | Servings: 3)

NUTRITIONAL INFO PER SERVING:

Calories: 380, Protein: 16g, Carbs: 4g, Fats: 19g

INGREDIENTS:

3 Eggs

5 tbsp Cottage Cheese

½ cup Cream Cheese

4 tbsp Sugar

½ tsp Vanilla Extract

DIRECTIONS:

1. Place all of the ingredients in a mixing bowl. Beat with an electric mixer for a few minutes, until soft and smooth. Divide the mixture between 3 mason jars. Seal.
2. Preheat the Sous Vide to 175 degrees F. Immerse the jars inside the bath. Cook for 90 minutes. Chill until ready to serve.

Coffee Buttery Bread

(Prep + Cook Time: 3 hours 10 minutes | Servings: 4)

NUTRITIONAL INFO PER SERVING:

Calories: 410, Protein: 5g, Carbs: 20g, Fats: 35g

INGREDIENTS:

6 ounces White Bread

¾ cup Butter

6 tbsp Coffee

½ tsp Cinnamon

1 tsp Brown Sugar

DIRECTIONS:

1. Slice the bread into strips and place in a Ziploc bag.
2. Whisk the other ingredients in a bowl and pour the mixture over the bread

3. Get rid of the excess air and seal the bag.
4. Preheat the Sous Vide water to 195 degrees F.
5. Place the bag inside.
6. Cook for 3 hours.

Carrot Muffins

(Prep + Cook Time: 3 hours 20 minutes | Servings: 10)

NUTRITIONAL INFO PER SERVING:

Calories: 173, Protein: 4g, Carbs: 11g, Fats: 12g

INGREDIENTS:

1 cup Flour

3 Eggs

½ cup Butter

¼ cup Heavy Cream

2 Carrots, grated

1 tsp Lemon Juice

1 tbsp Coconut Flour

¼ tsp Salt

½ tsp Baking Soda

DIRECTIONS:

1. Whisk the wet ingredients in one bowl and combine the dry ones in another.
2. Gently combine the two mixtures together.
3. Set your Sous Vide to 195 degrees F.
4. Divide the mixture between 5 mason jars (Do not fill more than halfway. Use more jars if needed).
5. Seal and immerse in the water. Cook for 3 hours. Cut into halves and serve.

Conclusion

Sous vide method is all about the simplicity through perfect texture and exquisite aroma of your food. It was my deepest desire to create a cookbook that will transform your everyday recipes into a rich heavenly meal that will gather your family around the table and create some precious memories.

A collection of easy meals come in a whole new form of the perfection of preparation, excellent taste, and mouthwatering aromas. This cookbook offers various combinations for every occasion – fancy dinner party, delicious and simple lunch, or a quick breakfast. Mastering this easy cooking technique will make you a kitchen hero, and soon enough you will start preparing some culinary classics like perfect beefsteak, chicken thighs, and lean vegetable stews. And the best part? You will no longer fear cooking for your loved ones. Sous vide will give you the same meal every single time!

Cooking is about family and food is all about eating healthy. The healthier and tastier your meal is, the happier your life will be. Dishes included in this sous vide cookbook are simple, delicious, and give you so many options that you'll be preparing them for years to come!

Have a wonderful time trying these recipes.

37887786R00060

Made in the USA
Middletown, DE
03 March 2019